MORE THAN
A MISSION STATEMENT

MORE THAN

HOW TO
ENHANCE CULTURE
TO CREATE
QUALITY GROWTH

THAN

A MISSION

STATEMENT

FRANK ROTELLO
BRENT BERNARDI

Advantage | Books

Published by Advantage, Charleston, South Carolina.
Member of Advantage Media.

ADVANTAGE is a registered trademark, and the Advantage colophon is a trademark of Advantage Media Group, Inc.

Printed in the United States of America.

10 9 8 7 6 5 4 3 2 1

ISBN: 978-1-64225-774-8 (Hardcover)
ISBN: 978-1-64225-773-1 (eBook)

Library of Congress Control Number: 2023904264

Cover design by Lance Buckley.
Layout design by Lance Buckley.

This publication is designed to provide accurate and authoritative information in regard to the subject matter covered. It is sold with the understanding that the publisher is not engaged in rendering legal, accounting, or other professional services. If legal advice or other expert assistance is required, the services of a competent professional person should be sought.

Advantage Media helps busy entrepreneurs, CEOs, and leaders write and publish a book to grow their business and become the authority in their field. Advantage authors comprise an exclusive community of industry professionals, idea-makers, and thought leaders. Do you have a book idea or manuscript for consideration? We would love to hear from you at **AdvantageMedia.com**.

We have been blessed to collaborate with great people and be mentored by outstanding leaders during our careers. The opportunities we were provided and experience we gained positioned us for success at Alpha. Our mentors were both internal at Barber-Colman, Siebe/Invensys, and across the country and throughout the world in the field offices and businesses that we had the opportunity to work with and support. The list is too long to write out, but please understand that we know who each person is and appreciate the positive impact they have had on our lives. Thank you to all of these amazing professionals and really good people.

We have always believed in paying it forward, and that will continue.

CONTENTS

INTRODUCTION

Moss doesn't grow on us. If there's something that we feel is the right thing to do, we take action. That's how Alpha Controls & Services was born.

But our story really begins at the Barber-Colman company, a large manufacturing company in Rockford, Illinois. Barber-Colman was founded in 1894 by Howard Colman and W. A. Barber. Colman was the inventor and entrepreneur, while Barber provided the initial financing with an investment of one hundred dollars. Through Howard Colman's innovation, they used that money to build a successful domestic and international company with thousands of patents in the textile, small motors and gears, machine tools, industrial instruments, aerospace, and commercial controls industries.

The two of us were on the corporate end but came up on two different sides of the commercial controls business; our careers were always on an odd parallel path. That included having a front-row seat when the family who ran the company decided to get out of the business and put together the ultimate succession plan. They were looking for buyers, and Siebe was a British conglomerate on an acquisition binge at the time, so Siebe purchased the company in 1987. Siebe eventually renamed the company Invensys after a merger with British Tire & Rubber.

"Nothing's gonna change." That's what management always says during any merger or acquisition, but that couldn't be further from the truth. Everything's going to change. It's just a matter of when. It started with two leadership changes within a year after acquiring the company. Siebe operated under a holding company structure and continued acquiring new companies to grow the business, so everything became about the numbers. Financial targets were set at the corporate level and driven into individual business units. As time went on, there was more short-term focus on results to maximize the stock price instead of considering what was best in the long term for the individual business units and their customers. Meanwhile there were several more leadership changes over that period that required constant reorganization. It led to instability that impacted the employees, distribution networks, and customers.

We saw the writing on the wall and knew it was the beginning of the end. It became apparent that Invensys just wanted to be in manufacturing and distribution. The owners wanted to focus on their core strengths and not take the risk required to grow the branch business. It became official in September 2002 when they issued a press release to announce they were selling the twenty-two branch contracting operations. Looking back, it was the right decision because it allowed them to better achieve their corporate objective and provide a significant opportunity to all the stakeholders.

This also created quite an opportunity for anyone who wanted to grasp it and take a chance on being in the contracting business. The two of us had reached a fork in the road. We could keep going down this same path doing things the same way, or we could become entrepreneurs, purchase some of these branches ourselves, and start doing things our way. Those parallel paths we had been on throughout our careers were about to converge.

2

BRENT

I was in desperate need of a lifestyle change. That was the primary reason I was first interested in purchasing the branches. I started at Barber-Colman a few days after I graduated from Bradley University in 1984. By 2002 I had become the general manager of North America, traveled worldwide, and logged about 1.5 million airline miles. The experience was phenomenal, but with three kids at home, I missed the family. Sure, I could take a job elsewhere, but that would require moving. We wouldn't have to move if I ran a local business, and I could be home every night.

The wheels started to turn in my head, but I needed to test the waters with my wife, Susie, before I did anything. When I got home, I happened to catch her when she was making dinner for the kids. I explained the situation, and before I even had a chance to tell her what I was thinking, she said, "Good! We'll buy the Rockford branch."

It was so automatic that she didn't even look up from the stove. I wasn't expecting her to be on board immediately, but I still felt I needed to warn her. "You know this is going to be pretty expensive, right?"

"We'll sell the house. We can buy another one later."

"No, no, no. We're not going to sell the house."

She put the spatula down and told me, "Then we're not going to screw this up."

"I don't plan on it."

"Then what's the problem?"

"I guess we need approval."

"You better work on that."

She went back to cooking for the kids, and whatever concerns I might have had quickly disappeared. I was confident, but I knew that I needed more than just the Rockford branch to make this work—I would need to purchase two. There was a branch in Chicago, but the bigger markets didn't operate the same way or value the same things. The Springfield, Illinois, branch would be a much better cultural fit even though it was further away, so that became the second one I targeted.

I also knew that I couldn't do this alone. After working with many of these independent companies trying to rebuild their trust in the corporation over the years since the acquisition, I had gotten to know some of the owners quite well. And I saw a pattern. The most successful ones had business partners with shared goals who believed in the same thing and were willing to take on some risk so that the organization could grow. I knew that I needed a business partner who shared my same vision, but you have to be careful when you pick a business partner or even ask someone to come on board as a partner.

> The most successful ones had business partners with shared goals who believed in the same thing and were willing to take on some risk so that the organization could grow.

Frank Rotello was always in the front of my mind. Why Frank? Who else? We had worked on two different sides of the company—me on the engineering and marketing side and Frank in finance and management on the branch side—but over the past three years, there were times during product launches and attempts to reorganize when we worked more closely together. We didn't have a personal relationship—we never went out for a beer together or anything like that. Most of our conversations revolved around solving problems in the business, but the more we talked, the more I could tell that our ideas about management, ownership, and risk lined up.

We thought the same way and believed in the same things, so we kept landing in the same place, and there was never any contention between us. Our conversations were almost too easy to have. More significantly, Frank was 100 percent trustworthy. I watched him treat people with respect, and he was always willing to professionally say the tough things when they needed to be said. When it came to someone with expertise, Frank had already done this many times over in the 1980s during his work with our joint ventures. Those joint ventures acted like independent companies, exposing him to phenomenal people who thought outside the box. And he became close with many of those people because he helped set them up in business. I couldn't ask for a business partner with more experience and qualifications than Frank Rotello. I knew that we would be a great complement to each other; I just had no idea if he was even interested.

By October 2002 the company was just starting the process of selling the branches when I found myself with Frank at Sea-Tac International Airport in Seattle. I told him what I was planning and asked, "Have you ever thought about doing this?"

"Yes! I've always thought about doing this."

"Well, do you wanna be partners—"

He answered before I could even finish asking the question: "I'm in!"

FRANK

I can still see us sitting in that elevator lobby on the fifth floor of the Marriott at Sea-Tac. We had flown in from Rockford, Illinois, that morning, so we had been up a long time, and we continued to stay up late into the night hammering out the details of a plan.

Until then, I had been so focused on selling the branches for the organization. I was putting teams together and trying to meet tight deadlines. A lot was going on, so I hadn't thought about venturing out on my own, but as soon as Brent mentioned it, it made perfect sense. *Why didn't I think of that?* We were each on board and 100 percent committed, so all that was left to figure out was how we would pull this off.

At Invensys we had worked with quality people and considered bringing someone else on board but ultimately decided that multiple partners wouldn't work. It would be just the two of us. I was already in the middle of selling these branches, so we first had to get approval from Invensys to buy Rockford and Springfield. We had to do it quickly, so there would be no conflicts of interest. We also had to make sure that we retained the employees while selling the branches, which meant having to communicate as openly as possible.

The more Brent and I talked at Sea-Tac, the more we saw that this would work. It got later and later into the night, but we were running on adrenaline by that point. The fact that everything came together so seamlessly and that we worked so well together made it that much more exciting.

I had twenty-five years of experience with Invensys. My first twelve years were in accounting and senior financial management. The remainder of my career was spent in branch management, national operations, and general management. I'd gotten my CPA but did not want to pursue a career in public accounting. I only got into accounting to understand the financial side of the business world. I never wanted to be an accountant for life. That's why, during my career, I transitioned into management, where I worked for twelve years, but what I really wanted to do was own a business. I had just turned fifty, and it looked like I was finally going to make that dream a reality. There were just a few more things we had to hammer out.

Before we left Seattle, I told Brent, "We've got to work on financing."

"I got that covered," he told me.

"How do you have that covered already?"

BRENT

I had been at the Invensys Classic golf tournament in Las Vegas one week earlier. The guest I invited was the owner of a partner business like ours who had several offices in Pennsylvania and was already in the process of buying the Philadelphia and Orlando branches the company was selling. Once he became successful, he wanted to help others, so he stepped up and paid it forward. He would bring the young people in those organizations under his umbrella and teach them to become more entrepreneurial before letting them buy him out.

Neither of our wives had made the trip, so we spent the week playing golf, bumming around, and going out to eat. I hadn't been able to attend the tournament the previous two years, so I looked forward to the experience. It proved to be a great week—we even got the chance to get a lesson from Tiger Wood's coach, Butch Harmon, who was there at the club for the tournament.

As if that day couldn't get any better, we left that practice round at the Rio Secco Golf Club on the bus with the rest of the crew when he said to me, "Please tell me that you're buying some of these companies you're selling." We had worked closely together, so he understood exactly what I had been going through at Invensys.

"There are only a couple of people who know this, and I trust you to keep it private, but yes. Rockford and Springfield."

"How are you financing it?"

"I need to work on that part. I've been talking to some banks and investment people, but I think I'll be good."

"No, that's not how that's going to work," he told me.

I had no idea what he was talking about. "What does that mean?"

"I'm going to finance you."

"You?"

"You have no idea how much you helped me over the years with my business."

"I was just doing my job."

"That's true. And now I'm going to do my job and help you. When you're done negotiating, just let me know how much you need, and I'll write you a check."

What happened after that was a blur. All I remember is looking him in the eye and saying, "You know, I'm going to cry now. This stuff doesn't happen."

"Yes, it does," he told me. "But I do have terms."

That's when I thought the other shoe was about to drop.

"I want no interest. I want no say or control within your company. You write the terms of repaying, and I'm good."

"What?" I was shocked. I couldn't believe what I was hearing. "I would love for you to coach and help."

"Oh, I'll do that, but I don't want to be on any boards or anything. You're going to have control of this."

He is a prime example of someone who became very successful and shared that success with others. We thanked him profusely and made sure to carve out room in our financial plan to pay him back with interest.

Frank and I were blessed from the beginning.

FRANK

My wife Janet wasn't as optimistic about the venture as Susie. "You're fifty," she told me. "You have a corporate job and are finally in a good spot."

"Yeah, but I have to travel everywhere, and if I move up in the organization, I'll only have to travel more. Wouldn't it be great to control our destiny?"

She wasn't discouraging, but with three kids at home, I knew that she was a little concerned. However, I had been managing these businesses for almost twenty years, and a good chunk of my career up to that point involved trying to improve the profitability, efficiency, and operations at these branches that we would be taking over. I knew we could be incredibly successful with the right people and business plan. I had done my due diligence. I had looked at this and run the numbers from every angle possible, and knowing the business as much as I did, there was minimal risk. Having worked with the branches and joint ventures, I knew we had all the employees and the right teams in place. We had a phenomenal customer base in these markets that had been with the branches forever. We just had to maintain that positive message to our customers. We'd also be reinvesting in the community because we were a locally owned and run company, not a big corporate entity with no ties or loyalty to the community.

The way I saw it, the worst-case scenario was that if this didn't work, I would go get a job elsewhere. Invensys would have probably hired me back. More than anything else, what concerned me was being able to pay back the initial loan. We had someone with enough confidence to give us the money to start the business, so we needed to make good on his generosity.

I had been around long enough to know that opportunities such as this one, where a major corporation was looking to divest out of a business that was already properly managed, rarely come along. It wasn't about luck. You have to be prepared to seize those opportunities, and nobody was as prepared as we were to do that at the time. We would have been crazy not to take advantage of it.

Of course when we brought our proposal to Invensys corporate, they thought we were the ones who were nuts. "Are you sure you guys really wanna do this?"

They had to ask, but they fully supported us and said yes to the sale. That final week in October was when we worked hard to finalize everything. We had a whole team of phenomenal people and used the same criteria we did with everyone else when selling the other branches. We had to renegotiate our deal so there weren't any conflicts, and Invensys had the final say, but they gave us a lot of latitude, and everything came together quickly because even they saw the opportunity.

> You have to be prepared to seize those opportunities, and nobody was as prepared as we were.

Brent and I expected to succeed and grow the business from the beginning. We're both super competitive and grew up playing sports—me football and Brent tennis. As former athletes, we always expect to win. You have to. You can't be afraid to lose or let your guard down because someone always wants to beat you. Of course nobody wins every time. Losing is a part of life, and nobody likes to lose, but when it does happen, you have to come back and ask, "Why didn't we win?" and "What do we need to do to improve, so we can win next time?" You have to pivot and adjust. That's the only way you will succeed in sports, and it's the same with business. That's how Brent and I approached this venture, and it's that attitude that has helped us win most of the time.

Approval was granted, the sale went through, and it was official. Brent always wanted to run a business, and I always wanted to own a business. I had spent most of my career struggling to get our branches around the country to leverage the best practices I had seen work.

Now we would get that chance and see if we were as smart as we thought and if these practices we believed in would help our organization grow. The ball was in our court. We had to run with it.

OUR UNIFIED VISION

The way you control the temperature in a building is to pump fifty-five-degree air into it and heat that air to create the desired environment. On the surface that sounds simple, but a lot of outside factors can make that task more difficult, the weather being the most obvious. A building doesn't know if it's winter or summer.

Our job is to install the equipment and utilize technology to maintain a consistent temperature and humidity, so our customers' buildings are comfortable, secure, and efficient. We do that in several different ways, primarily through HVAC equipment like air handlers, rooftop units, electric reheats, hot water reheats, and boilers and chillers for heating and cooling. We tie in lighting and do some metering and power management as well. This gets more complicated when the customer is a university or a company with a campus environment that has dozens of buildings where the schedules and occupancy levels fluctuate, but no matter how big we grow or what type of job we take on, the formula for what we do remains the same.

We have been working together and running Alpha Controls & Services for almost two decades, so it's no surprise that we were on the same page from day one. Our perspectives might differ, but our core values have been aligned, and so has our message. We have the same expectations, management styles, and leadership qualities. Neither of us manages with a sharp tongue. We manage with direction, authority, and resolve. And we're both willing to take the risk for the organization to move forward. That's why we've been successful partners going into our twentieth year. Most partnerships don't last that long.

What follows is the story of our twenty-year journey. If you own a small business and want to see it grow, you can learn from what helped us do that. We could bore you with graphs and charts, but we feel our story is the best example, told by us, our employees, and examples of our customer interactions. We came into the business together. We built the business together. It's only appropriate that we tell our story and write this book together.

CHAPTER 1
WHAT IS CULTURE?

If you're trying to define culture, that's probably a good sign that you don't have it. Your belief system and your actions determine culture. It's your vision for what you want to do and how you want to accomplish it. You can't go out and buy culture. Culture is who you are, and we clearly understood who we were long before we started Alpha.

Back at Invensys, we were forced to deal with financial and structural issues at the branches. At one point we decided to step back and reevaluate the company's leadership, so we brought the entire management team into the office for a meeting on a Sunday afternoon. During that meeting we planned our future—how we were going to communicate and what our message was going to be. We were there for several hours but emerged having crafted a mission statement that outlined our commitment to helping our customers meet their business objectives and become successful.

When we left Invensys, we realized that nobody there had any use for that mission statement, so we adopted that statement as our own when we started Alpha. We had already created it. We believed everything we said, and it perfectly encapsulated our vision for the culture, so why not use it? We certainly weren't going to create a better one.

"Alpha Controls & Services is a team committed to enabling oppor-tunities by eliminating barriers through leveraging technology to assist our customers in achieving their business objectives."

It was simple. We set out to build a successful business, take care of our customers, and provide opportunities for our employees. That meant continuous change and continuous improvement.

That statement has guided and driven the business over the years, and it still rings true today. After almost twenty years, that statement remains a litmus test for us. If we're ever stuck or unsure, we ask ourselves if our actions align with that mission statement. If they do, it's the right thing for us to do.

Culture begins at the top with leadership—your core values and how you treat people. The result is the value you add for your customers and the opportunities you create for your employees. You either have that as a leader, or you don't, and you can't just say it or write it down on paper. You must genuinely believe it because you can't fool people. You can't say one thing and do something else. Your employees will see that, and you can't expect them to buy into a vision if the people who created the company aren't consistent and practicing what they preach. So the responsibility falls on your shoulders to set the tone, properly communicate what's expected, and lead by example because that's the only way to get everyone on board the same train and working together. For us, our directors and frontline people are the faces of the company because they are the ones who interact the most with the customer, not us, so it's crucial that they believe in that same value system and what we're trying to accomplish.

We demonstrated this from day one with every team member. When we interview prospective employees, we tell every single one of them that what they see is what they get. We try to be easy to talk to and down to earth, and we try to speak confidently about our goals without appearing to have an ego. We make it a point to be as genuine as possible so employees know that they aren't going to start work and suddenly see that we are different people. If they like what they see, believe in what they see, want to grow, improve, and work hard, they can be a good fit.

However, it's a two-way street. Because in exchange for that effort and commitment to the vision, we invest in their training, development, and growth to create opportunities. Our employees must perform and add value to the company because if we can't grow, we can't continue to provide those opportunities. During that process, adaptability is important. They have to be willing to recognize when something isn't working and pivot when necessary, but the one thing they can't compromise on is that core belief system as laid out in our mission statement because culture is a direct result of that belief system. When faced with a difficult decision, you must return to that belief system. That's what we need to build a successful company, and it's been one of the keys to our success. However, we wouldn't know that or be where we are today without our experience. That prevented us from making some of the other mistakes that commonly prevent new businesses from becoming successful.

LEARNING FROM THE PAST

As people, we learn through our successes and failures—we also learn through the successes and failures of others. Our experience at Invensys, as mentioned in the introduction, taught us a series of lessons that neither of us would trade for anything because when it came time for us to venture out on our own, we had a much better understanding of what kind of company we wanted to build.

Invensys was not native to our industry, so when they took over, they attempted to merge different related technology companies to benefit from the greater business synergy. That's when things began to change quickly on the corporate side, and there was a significant lack of stability since there was always new management above us. Some left voluntarily, some not so voluntarily. We used to joke that our job was to train our bosses, but it wasn't really a joke. Corporate was always bringing in someone from the outside who didn't understand the cadence and details of the business. That's significant when you've got independent distributors and wholesale organizations while selling to manufacturers in OEM businesses and running branches. There were pretty diverse requirements within the organization.

While operating in this new system at Invensys, everything had to be done by the book. Decisions were made based on quarterly reports with an eye toward what would impact the company's stock value. They focused on headcounts and put stipulations on us because the inherent corporate belief was that organizations don't act responsibly and that people don't do the right thing when given a choice.

They also believed that anyone could do the job, and, worse, people were expendable. So if we had two people doing two facets of a similar job, they wanted only one person doing it and would make that cut without changing the process, leveraging technology, or adjusting things up and down the organization to accommodate that change. No matter what you were doing, they assumed you could be doing it better, and the best way to achieve that in their mind was to cut some heads. We saw that happen year after year after year, but it was never done responsibly or with a disciplined approach that took any of the consequences or tradeoffs into consideration, so they could never maintain the same productivity, performance, or results.

We were forced to implement these decisions while managing our employees and customers, but we couldn't train and develop people how we would have liked, so we couldn't execute as efficiently. Add to that the internal wasted effort within the bureaucracy that required reporting to middle management, and it used to drive us crazy because these decisions were being made on a high level by individuals who had completely lost sight of what was needed to serve the customer. That's the core function of any business, and you can't ever lose sight of your core function.

Much of what we were doing within a big corporation could be placed in two categories: what worked and what didn't. Given our position within the corporate structure, we also had a very clear understanding of *why* certain things worked and didn't. If we could take advantage of that experience and those lessons, we knew we could build Alpha into something that would last.

From the very beginning, our goal was to modernize our process and our business to do more with what we had, not the same with less. We always wanted to do more. We also set out to eliminate the inefficiency associated with bureaucratic middlemen. We would promptly get our team members the information and data they needed to bring their respective projects in on time. We weren't going to build any additional management layers into our organization, and we sure as hell weren't going to micromanage. Instead we would hold our employees accountable so they could manage themselves. We sought to create a proactive organization where employees could anticipate problems and make changes.

> *We weren't going to build any additional management layers into our organization, and we sure as hell weren't going to micromanage.*

It all looked terrific on paper, but transitioning from a large international corporation with hundreds of people reporting to us to a small business proved quite a change. It was a different cadence. And to be honest, it took us a little while to adapt because we had to start from scratch. We left a corporate environment where all these systems were in place and entered into a small business environment with no systems. We also didn't have the luxury of time, so things had to move quickly. However, because of our experience and network, these weren't completely uncharted waters.

Years earlier, when searching for a software company to replace our system at Invensys, we contacted Jonas Construction out of Toronto. The owner wrote every bit of code. Jonas was one of three companies we shortlisted at the time for Invensys, but Invensys wanted us to go with another company. But when we went back to look at Jonas for Alpha, it proved to be a perfect fit. Jonas's system was scalable, so you could run it with a $1 million business or a $50 million business. We knew that we could build our business around it, so we made the investment.

Susan Koneval and Vickie Hilker left Invensys to join Alpha and were the first two business administrators we hired. Both Susan and Vickie were instrumental in leveraging their industry knowledge and experience to help with the initial startup of the business. Once we got payroll and billings in order, we focused on creating a solid benefits package. Even though we were a small business, we were competing against the Invensys benefit package and all our other major competitors. We had to retain our talent, so we certainly couldn't ask our employees to take a step backward regarding benefits. That's when we received a lot of help from a local bank that set up a line of credit and 401(k) benefit plans. They also brought in a local company to set up Alpha's insurance benefits. We were able to make the right decisions because the expertise, experience, and knowledge gained at the corporate level helped us mitigate the risk. There was a plan B, but luckily, we never had to go there.

STEADY GROWTH FROM DAY ONE

May 19, 2003, was Alpha's first official day of business, and we were off and running. We knew many people at the Rockford and Spring-field branches, especially the senior people, because we had worked with many of them for twenty years, and we got to know them all much better during those first couple of years. We frequently made the three-hour drive to Springfield. Sometimes we stayed over, and sometimes we made it back home in time for dinner that same night. That was six hours in the car, and people thought we were crazy, but it was still better than flying around the country. Those six-hour trips became fewer and farther between as we learned how to leverage technology and divide and conquer. More importantly our team members were stepping up and taking ownership of the relationships and business actions.

We had such a strong customer base. Barber-Colman had a strong brand in northern and central Illinois. The branches had done a good job of getting systems sold, so there was a solid customer base in both markets that had been with us for years. Most of our business was the backlog that came with the branch; after that first year, we were a $6.7 million business. The following year we set out to leverage new technologies to move forward and expand our offerings.

Invensys had only sold us the contracting piece of the business, not its service business that would let us maintain and repair the equipment we install. However, we knew that it wasn't practical for Invensys to maintain its service business and have it coexist with the new independent businesses operating in the same market. So, four months after purchasing the branches, we acquired the service business by hiring the employees and purchasing the inventory and tools required to support it. Those two components brought the organization together and paved the way for future growth opportunities.

In the beginning we were partnered with Invensys to provide all the products and technologies we deployed. Invensys was acquired by Schneider Electric in 2006, which opened up a whole new world for us. It's been a mutually beneficial relationship that helped us to grow. Schneider Electric is recognized as an industry leader and has become such a valuable asset. We are now what's called a Master EcoXpert partner with Schneider Electric, which puts us in some great company within our industry. We have specific territorial responsibilities when implementing the EcoStruxure building operation solutions. We're Schneider's avenue to the marketplace in those territories, but we believe our partnership goes beyond being a value-added reseller of its technology. We like to think of ourselves as collaborators because we also service its solutions afterward, so we work with people on all levels of the organization.

Our employees receive a lot of technical support and training from Schneider on its equipment. We budget and benchmark how much time we spend on training and how that can translate to productive billable hours on the job. Being able to reach and often exceed that goal is what allows our younger employees to be as productive as some veterans. Because we have such quality young people who can step up and into an ongoing project when someone gets pulled away, something else takes priority, or an emergency arises, we can rely on each phase of our projects being managed effectively and coming in on time and on budget. We now test some of Schneider's products and provide feedback before they come to market. This applies to the service and software programs as well. It really has become a true partnership.

There were other key pivot points over the next few years where we won competitive projects and proved that we could deliver at a high level, so we gained recognition. We had some great customers who were demanding at times, and we experienced growing pains, but that forced us to work together to address the areas where we needed to improve, and we became a stronger organization as a result. By 2008 we had grown to become a $12 million business, and because we had such a solid backlog, we could continue to grow and add to our team while our competitors were holding even. In 2019 and 2020, we experienced double-digit growth—we even grew through the COVID-19 pandemic. Growth is in our DNA because we're impatient and never satisfied, so we're constantly challenging ourselves and looking for ways to be more efficient. However, we make sure that it's "quality growth" because we don't want to get too far out in front of our skis.

We're in the construction industry, and while we're a specialty contractor, what's different about us is that we are two individuals with extensive corporate experience. In contrast, most business owners in this industry start in the field before evolving into leadership, and then a small percentage goes into ownership. We benefit from never entering the business to take on a specific role other than leadership, team building, and trying to grow the business.

> *So many business owners look only at what's on their desks and live day to day. They're working in the business, not on the business.*

Because of our professional upbringing, we naturally approach business differently. We were always responsible for more than the success of just a singular team. At one point we controlled twenty-seven diverse businesses across two countries. We have become hardwired to look at the bigger picture. So many business owners look only at what's on their desks and live day to day. They're working *in* the business, not *on* the business. They never take a step back to look at the situation from thirty thousand feet. Even initially we were focused on the long term and were willing to sacrifice instant gratification if we saw the benefit a year or two down the road.

Often, when people need to work on their business, they must first work on themselves. It might not be natural for folks used to performing a specific critical function within a business to step back and say, "I need to do my job differently." It's hard for anyone to do that because it's not how we're built. We are all products of our environment, but what's required to truly create and sustain a winning business is to make changes and take different approaches to see how they turn out—like a sailboat that needs to tack when the wind shifts. There will always be something that will force you to adjust because stability doesn't exist. The ground beneath you is constantly moving, no matter what, so you must learn how to create stability. For us that meant continually having to reengineer and modernize our business so we could continue serving our customers by using our services to help them provide comfortable, safe, and secure working and living environments for their customers and employees. The more we invested in that, the faster the business grew. It's not always natural to think like that or look at things from that perspective if you haven't had to do it before.

Looking back now, did we accomplish what we set out to do in 2002? Is the world a better place because Alpha exists? If you look at the customers we've helped, the impact we've had on our employees, and what we've been able to give back to the community, we must be doing something right, so the answer has to be yes. While our experience within the industry allowed us to create the company's systems and infrastructure, another significant component of our success was the culture, which is the lifeblood of any organization. We would not be where we are today had we not established a strong company culture from the beginning, but it's one thing to talk about it, and it's another thing to live it. Those two don't always go hand in hand, so it requires being intentional.

RETURNING TO THE ALPHA FAMILY
By Dan Newkirk: Director of Energy Engineering

My grandfather was an aircraft controls mechanic, and my dad worked in industrial controls. They both did engineering-related work, but neither was a professional engineer with a degree. I appreciated that lineage, and following in their footsteps was important to me, so I earned my master's in mechanical engineering and technology from Purdue University in 2014. I had initially pursued a master's thesis, so I appreciated the research and academic path that would lead me to earn my PhD, but that direction felt like it would have left me out on an island. I wanted to work somewhere with more of a team environment where I could use my engineering background within the industry.

I was hired by Alpha after graduating college in 2014, and for the first four years, I gained valuable in-person experience. I had worked an internship in college, but I was brand-new to the industry and still had a lot to learn. That in-person experience accelerated my learning curve. In 2018 my wife completed her PhD from the University of Illinois, and we relocated to Ohio, where she had accepted a tenure-track position. Alpha was incredible and allowed me to continue in my role remotely.

This was back when working from home wasn't as common as it was after the pandemic, so I couldn't help but feel isolated and never genuinely adapted to this hybrid work-life model.

Over the next year and a half, I earned my professional engineering license. That was a big milestone, and I still felt that pull to do more professional engineering work for a consulting firm, so I started exploring my options. Because I was working from home and living in a different state, I think Frank and Brent knew that I might have been looking for a job elsewhere. When I told them I needed to resign, they understood because they knew what getting that professional engineering license meant to me. After landing a consulting role at an engineering firm, I had a going-away dinner with Frank and Brent, and they told me, "If you ever want to come back, let us know and we can work it out." Most people who leave a job don't experience that, and to part ways on such great terms was a testament to our relationship over the years.

I quickly discovered that consulting engineering wasn't quite what I imagined it to be. When working on the contract side with Alpha, I was getting paid to install and build things while directly involved with the energy-efficiency projects. The consulting role was more about giving advice on energy efficiency without actually doing it. That's when I realized I wanted to be back on the other side where I was with Alpha, so I could make the customer's buildings more energy efficient, not just offer advice.

By 2020 we were in the middle of the pandemic, and everything had changed, especially how technology allowed many people to work from home. That hybrid work-life model I had struggled with initially didn't seem so foreign anymore. There had been a massive shift in the culture. Meanwhile I had been in contact with people from Alpha regularly. When I was in Rockford, I popped in to say hi to Brent and Frank. I talked to my old boss Jason every three to six months to see how things were going and find out what was happening in the industry. When I learned they were hiring, even though the position wasn't exactly what I was looking for, it started the discussion of what I wanted to do and how I could use my professional engineering license. I was looking at other places and had received multiple offers, but I loved the people at Alpha, and we found a position that worked well for everyone. That tipped the scales in favor of Alpha, and I decided to return to the company.

I currently lead our energy engineering team and focus on making our customers' buildings more energy efficient. To their credit, the people at Alpha have been super supportive of me throughout the twists and turns in my career and life in general. But that's all part of the Alpha culture. It goes beyond coworkers being friendly to each other and involves coworkers being friends. It's why I remained in touch with Jason, Brent, and Frank after I was gone and why we could find a position that fit both our needs when I expressed interest in coming back. It's great to be part of a team again. Brent and Frank always use the term "Alpha family," and that's what it feels like to me. There is a deep sense of camaraderie that is important in the construction industry because there is a lot that can go wrong. Knowing that people on your team are there when something unexpected happens is incredibly important and has been a significant part of my experience with the company.

HOW WE STAY ON MISSION

You can talk about your mission, write it down, and try to instill those beliefs and values in your employees, but how can you tell if it's working? Results are the ultimate barometer, but if you were to break it down even further, we've discovered three key tenets that we continually rely on to help guide us so we remain on mission.

#1. FAIRNESS

If we could boil our mission statement down to a single word, it would be "fairness." That's what governed us from the beginning and what we strive to achieve with everything we do. We treat our employees and customers fairly and expect them to treat us fairly in return. It's that simple. If we're going to look someone in the eye and ask a tough question, we have to know that we're fair to them.

We also have to make sure we are being fair to ourselves. If a customer wants us to do something for free, we must first look at ourselves to determine what's fair and ask, "Have we done our job correctly up to that point?" and "Is this something they should be paying for?" If not, we need to look at that customer and say, "If we do this for free, it's not fair to our organization, and it's not fair to our relationship because we're adding financial value to your business."

That's what we do, and it works. That word, "fairness," has continued to guide us throughout the years. That's what we teach our employees, and we hold them accountable to remain fair. If they are frustrated with a customer, we tell them to take a step back and ask themselves, "Am I being fair?" They may not always be happy with their answer, but it gets them thinking differently.

#2. OPEN LINES OF COMMUNICATION

To be genuinely fair requires everyone to come to an understanding and communicate openly. If an employee comes to us claiming another employee disrespected them, we will look at the root of the problem. What exactly happened? Was someone being unprofessional, unreasonable, or unfair, or did the employee just not like what the other person had to say? That's a critical distinction because there is a big difference between disrespect and two people with different ideas seeing things from different perspectives. The former is a problem, but the latter makes an organization stronger. If you listen and keep an open mind, those types of discussions can be incredibly productive, and we'd go so far as to say they are required to grow.

The two of us don't always agree. We often see the same situation or a challenge from a slightly different perspective. If this occurs in front of the group, sometimes we'll even stop what we're doing and say, "Hold on, folks. The two of us need to talk about this."

Whenever we disagree on perspective, we can always find common ground if we talk it out because our perspectives, albeit different at times, complement each other. The fact that we can sometimes see a situation or challenge differently means that the company benefits from two perspectives instead of one. That leaves the door open for a discussion, which can sometimes result in a better way to do things that we would not have stumbled upon had we been in lockstep agreement regarding everything. That's why communication is so important.

#3. TEAMWORK

If you're tasked with pushing a giant boulder up a hill, one person can't do it alone. It requires a team operating like one cohesive unit with the same agenda and objective. Teamwork is the result when a strong culture is instilled because everyone is on the same page, can communicate openly with respect, and can work together to find a solution.

This is another area where we try to lead by example. Some business partners wake up and immediately find themselves on the same lily pad. You have other partners who wake up on their own lily pad but find they can easily hop back and forth as needed, and that's the way we operate. On any given day, either of us can easily hop over to the other guy's lily pad to help with a particular job, even if it requires us to get a little bit out of our comfort zone.

The reality is that things will not always run smoothly and will never be perfect. You know that you've created a robust and self-sustaining team when its members know they have the freedom to make mistakes. Knowing that you aren't going to get reprimanded or fired for making a mistake takes the pressure off, but there is one crucial caveat. You need to learn from that mistake to grow, move forward, and not make it again. We all make mistakes, but learning from those mistakes makes us better. Much of our entire company has been created by learning from the mistakes of others.

> *Establishing culture is one thing—maintaining it while you continue to grow is another.*

Establishing culture is one thing—maintaining it while you continue to grow is another. We learned that firsthand as we grew over the years and expanded into four different offices across two states. Change is unavoidable and a prerequisite if you want to grow, but how can you ensure that your company culture doesn't change as a result? As time passes it's natural that some people will leave the organization, and you will have to bring new people in. How can you instill that same value system in those new leaders? How do you reinforce those core cultural values and beliefs on all levels, so you can continue to experience growth?

To answer those questions, we turn to what we have used to guide us from the beginning—our mission statement, and we work to develop what we consider our number one asset—our employees.

COMMITMENTS AND VALUES

Customer	Employees	Performance	Teamwork	Technology
° #1 Priority ° Solve problems ° Exceed expectations ° Cultivate loyal customers ° Trusted Advisor	° Most important asset ° Open communication ° Mutual respect ° Investment in development ° Safety ° Compensation & profit sharing	° Set and communicate goals and objectives ° Expect success— winning attitude ° Measure results ° Learn from mistakes, move on! ° Continuous improvement ° Share in company success	° Focus on internal and external customers ° Take ownership ° Focus on results ° Commitment to the team ° Celebrate team successes	° Invest ° Efficiency ° Effectiveness ° Leverate technology to help Alpha and our customers meet their business objectives

CHAPTER 2
PEOPLE ARE JUST PEOPLE

W e once brought in an outside consultant to coach our employees, and during one exercise he asked everyone to brainstorm what was unique about Alpha and how we could position that within the company. It sounded like a good exercise on paper, but every single thing that was brought up was not unique to our company. Whether it was a technology or strategy, one of our competitors had used it at some point. The only thing our competition didn't have was our employees. That's it! Every business has competition and looks for ways to differentiate itself, but we know that no external factor can do that for us. What's going to set us apart has to be internal. We can't control what our competition does, but we can control how we treat our employees. So that's what we invest in and nurture to give us an advantage.

At corporate we were often assigned what felt like impossible tasks, but we had to put together the right team to execute that plan. As leaders in those situations, we had to take a positive approach. That meant supporting our team members but not pushing them so hard that they burned out. It also meant acknowledging that not everything was going to be perfect. But we learned that if your team members believe in you and what you're trying to accomplish, they go above and beyond. A team with focus, spirit, and trust (especially trust) will stop making excuses, hold each other accountable, and watch each other's backs. That gives them the confidence to do great things. These people have different perspectives, but if you get them working together toward a common goal, you can accomplish almost anything. That's why today we invest in our employees to provide them with the right resources, training, and systems to make their jobs easier, so they can do an excellent job for our customers. That's what makes all the difference. Our competitors can have the same processes and technology, but they don't have our people, which is why our employees are our number one asset.

From day one, we understood the importance of putting our employees before ourselves. When Invensys announced its decision to sell the branches, there was a lot of uncertainty and angst among the branch employees, and with good reason. Nobody really knew how the change would impact them. Having purchased Rockford and Springfield, we didn't want the employees to leave. They knew the customers and had worked to establish those relationships. We needed them to help us build the company we envisioned, so we tried to make their transition as smooth as possible. A key component of the Invensys plan to sell the branches was to create an incentive program with retention bonuses that required employees remain during the acquisition period. We knew we were asking a lot of our people, but we convinced many of the branch employees to stay on board, and we also brought some great people along with us from corporate. These employees were leaving what would have been stable jobs at Invensys for a couple of years at least, but they decided to take a leap of faith to join us at Alpha. That meant something to us, and we had to make sure we took care of them.

We can't stress enough how important our employees are to us, but we also know how important we are to them. The decisions we make and how we run the company will impact not only us, but also the ninety families we are responsible for today. We never forget that responsibility, and it's not one we ever take lightly.

FINDING THE RIGHT PEOPLE AND GETTING THEM IN THE RIGHT ROLES

When we opened for business on May 19, 2003, we had a blank slate and a clear idea of what we did and didn't want to do regarding employees. After coming from the typically understaffed corporate bureaucracy with many job descriptions and multiple salary grades, we knew we didn't want any of that.

A poster hung on the wall of our corporate attorney's office titled Peter's Law. One of the points in this so-called "Creed of the Sociopathic Obsessive Compulsive" stated, "Bureaucracy is a challenge to be conquered with a righteous attitude, a tolerance for stupidity, and a bulldozer when necessary." That became a guiding light of sorts for us because bureaucracy doesn't solve problems. We wanted to be lean and flat. That meant one clear and concise job description for each position.

That approach worked well initially, but as the company grew, we had to adopt some of that corporate hierarchy as we added more employees. If we wanted to maintain our vision and not devolve into the inefficient bureaucracy we despised, we knew that we had to build our company and team around our values—specifically our culture. We did that through communication. It was important that all our team members knew exactly where we were coming from. It was equally important that we understood where they were coming from. That began during the hiring process.

We work with all different personalities, but it doesn't matter if we're hiring a technically proficient design engineer, field engineer, programmer, installer, or a business development person who will communicate directly with the customer; we make sure we understand where they're coming from. We tell them that if they want to come on board, the position first has to be right for them. Second, our values and culture must align with their belief system. If they can check those two boxes, this will most likely be a good fit for them and their families. It's crucial that employees not overlook their families as the final component to ensure a good fit because the personal and professional experiences are connected more than people realize. Work life will always carry over into personal life and vice versa. It's inevitable. You can't ever put the company before your core belief system or your family because there will be an imbalance. But if the company's values align with your own, and the situation is right for your family, you will be a good fit for the company. That's been the basis for how we lead and hire for the past twenty years, but getting on the same page can be tricky.

The interview process is a beauty contest. Interviewees sit up straight and tend to say exactly what they believe we want to hear. Through years of trial and error and a few mistakes along the way, it's constantly evolving, but we received some sage advice that changed how we interviewed applicants. The key is not to rush the process and not to interview applicants together. Instead the two of us agree on a set of questions we want to ask, and then we ask that person the same questions over multiple days. If what someone tells us is not natural for them, their story will change over time. It goes back to the old adage that when you tell a lie, you will eventually have to tell another lie to cover up the original lie, but if you tell the truth, it will always be the truth, whether you like it or not. The same rule applies during the job interview process. If we take the time, we will eventually learn who these applicants really are, but we don't rely only on our impression. We've learned the benefit of bringing behavioral science into the equation. Having a defined process is critical, especially as we push the recruitment and hiring process down into the organization to the next level of supervision and leadership.

In 2015 we had a few retirements on the horizon and were simultaneously looking to expand the company while allowing our employees to rise from within. It was right around this time we learned about an assessment tool called the Culture Index from an executive forum group. It used analytics to more accurately determine if and where an individual might fit into our organization. By learning what interests and motivates people, we could avoid putting them in the wrong role. There is a science behind how people work that can't be overridden by will or desire. You can't stick someone in a position where they are not a good fit and expect them to succeed. You may win in the short term, but that's not a strategy for long-term success. This is true of new hires and of existing employees.

When we first started using the Culture Index, we did an audit of the entire company. That meant all our existing employees took the assessment to ensure they were in the right position for their skill set. It's possible to have the right people but in the wrong role because it doesn't match their strengths. If a person isn't a good fit for a specific role, it should be no surprise when they don't perform at an optimal level. Once our audit was completed, we laid out the profiles for all our employees in the conference room. Luckily none of our employees

It was just as crucial to understand and define our roles as it was to understand our people.

was a glaring mismatch for their role, but we did see some fascinating patterns. Management and business development tended to fit in one bucket and engineers in another. This information proved invaluable when looking at how we would promote from within and take the company in the new direction we wanted to go.

What was great about the Culture Index was that it forced us as a team to sit down and really formalize job descriptions and define what we truly needed in each position as we started to change the organization. It allowed us to put employees in roles where they could utilize their strengths, do what they enjoyed, and perform tasks aligned with their motivation. We want to give our employees the best opportunity to grow in a way that not only helps them serve our customers and add value to the company, but also accelerates their career paths.

We were once instructed by the Culture Index team that we had all the wrong people in a specific technical role. When we looked at the role, we realized we had all the right people, but the role wasn't correctly defined. That's when we realized that it was just as crucial to understand and define our roles as it was to understand our people. That way they can continue to grow and add value to the customer.

Employees only need to take this Culture Index assessment once. The results don't change over time. This is why we first administer it during the hiring process. Before we bring in anyone new, we have them submit a Culture Index assessment to determine if they would be a good fit for the position they're applying for. The Culture Index has proven to be a handy guide in learning the science of how a particular person works. That is a significant asset in the development and management of our teams.

ADAPTABILITY AND LEARNING HOW TO PAINT WITHIN THE LINES

Finding the right people for the right roles is the first step; acclimating them is the next. It takes time to learn our software tools, workflows, and technologies and use them in a way that adds value to our customers.

It doesn't matter what type of business you're in; when dealing with people, those people will give you results, which can be good or bad. Everyone is different, and not everyone starts from the same place. Pick three different people, and they might approach the same task from three completely different perspectives. Not everyone will be receptive and automatically fall in line with what you want to do. It sometimes requires a deft touch to motivate employees and get them to do things differently without ruffling any feathers.

This process of coaching people, bringing everyone up to speed, and getting them on the same page takes time and patience because very rarely will someone be able to do something correct right out of the gate. In fact it's dumb luck if someone gets it right the first time. Some might fumble through, but you must keep encouraging and coaching them. One of the biggest challenges is making it clear to them that it's okay to make a mistake. Mistakes are inevitable, but that's how we learn. They force you to step back and examine why you fell short. When you do that, there is no actual failure because it's a learning experience that forces you to improve. You're going to get worse before you get better. Picture any football or basketball team trying to set up new plays. They have to practice until one day it all clicks, and then they get it. When that happens, they are much better than they had ever been before. That's a feeling we've all experienced, and we know when it happens. It takes some people longer to get there than others, but they must go through the process of trying, failing, and succeeding.

We have high expectations for all our employees. We always have those conversations with new employees so they understand the next step and what's expected, but when we commit to new employees, they must commit to adding value to the organization by serving the customer and creating opportunities. That often requires them to move at a fast pace. It's necessary given some of the timetables and schedules for our jobs. After that initial breaking-in period, we tend to find out quickly if a new hire can adjust and keep up with that pace.

We know the culture is strong when our employees can root out these issues independently. When creating and sustaining the company culture, the message can't only come from us. The leaders must buy in and instill those values in those beneath them. Team members also need to hear it from their peers, and sometimes they put more pressure on each other than we would ever put on them. We've even had some employees tell us, "You need to fire that person." That only reiterates the importance of ensuring the lines of communication are open and that all employees are on board with the vision and the culture from the beginning, so everyone has something to rally around.

Whenever there is an issue within the organization, the one thing we don't do is point fingers. If a new employee struggles to adapt to the culture, we first look internally at ourselves before we look at the team members and start criticizing. No employee deliberately sets out to make a mistake, be disruptive, or create an issue, so we first ask ourselves, "What didn't we do from a coaching standpoint? What didn't we do from a training standpoint? What didn't we do from a leadership standpoint? Have we been fair and given them every opportunity?" Sometimes we have, and other times we haven't. And when we haven't, that's a mistake we need to rectify.

When it comes to rooting out these issues, feedback from our employees is essential. The caveat is that the feedback needs to be constructive and honest. We're not perfect, and we can't be aware of everything, so we must create an environment where the employees trust the people above them to give their honest opinion when something is wrong or could be done better. That allows us to make changes and give our employees the proper support and the answers they need.

Constructive feedback will also draw our attention to the little things that can easily be overlooked but create big ripples within an organization if unaddressed, especially as you're bringing new people in and trying to grow. We once hired a control tech who had an issue with health insurance and open enrollment. It seemed routine to us because it's the way we had always done things, but he was new to the organization, and he had just had a child, so it was a big issue for him. He was hired when we worked remotely, so we hadn't met him in person. When Frank finally met him during an employee meeting, he made it a point to go up and talk with the employee about the situation and get to know him better. Frank listened and communicated where we were coming from as a company. When it came down to it, we thought the situation was fair for both him and the company. He didn't particularly like the answer, but he accepted it. We might not have been able to give him everything he wanted, but we made sure to close the loop, and, if nothing else, that showed that we meant what we said. Even though our hands were tied with that particular issue, had we not tried to address the issue, that individual could have grown frustrated, and we could have lost a new employee over something as small as a benefit question that wasn't properly handled.

It's hard to do the little things when you're a big organization; even at our current size, every issue won't work its way up the ladder to us. As we grow we need to ensure that we have the right people and proper systems to continue handling those concerns that we might never be aware of. And even though we're building that leadership structure, we strive to create an environment where nobody should feel threatened if an employee brings a matter directly to us. What's most important to us is that nobody gets tuned out, and everyone knows that we will do our best to resolve the issue.

Unfortunately not every issue can get resolved, and not every employee can get on board or stay up to speed. Only after we've made sure an employee has had all the training and documentation required to prepare them for the situation can we look a team member in the eye and say the problem is on their end. We then try to figure out if it's an issue we can help them with or if they need to help themselves. If we've done everything possible to help that employee be successful and it still isn't working out, we must make the difficult decision to part ways. Unfortunately, we've had to let people go several times at Alpha, and it's one of the worst things we have to do. If there is a good or less painful way to do it, we aren't aware of it yet. It always stings for everyone involved, but if there is a problem, we must move on it quickly. The longer you put it off, the more stress you put on yourself, the organization, and the employee.

PROMOTING FROM WITHIN

We've never subscribed to the idea that we need to bring someone in from the outside to make improvements. There is a corporate mindset that if someone came from another company or a different industry, they would add more value than someone promoted from within. Nobody ever uttered those words, but the actions a company like Invensys took in the 1980s and 1990s clarified its philosophy. The Invensys higher-ups would consider promoting from within, but for leadership positions they tended to view the existing employees as a barrier and not a solution. They also assumed that someone from the outside would bring a unique approach that could significantly improve the business. Rarely did that ever work out.

There are some excellent and experienced people in our field we were able to bring in. These were talented people with great references. They often came from recruiters, so they arrived in this fancy package and appeared to be wrapped up perfectly with a beautiful bow, but once we unwrapped that package, we didn't always like what we saw. Sometimes that takes six months to become visible, and sometimes it's clear immediately. The main problem we find is that these new employees don't come in with the mindset that they will assimilate into our culture. They often arrive having worked for our competitors and are stuck in their ways, making it difficult for them to get on board with

> *We want someone interested in fitting in and being a part of the team, not someone who wants to run their own plays.*

what we're trying to do. With leaders like us, who are confident in the processes and systems we have implemented, we want someone interested in fitting in and being a part of the team, not someone who wants to run their own plays. That confidence and those systems got us where we are today, so if someone isn't on the same page, they're holding us back.

This doesn't mean that we can't get better or improve upon what we're doing. We don't know it all, so we listen to people and watch what they do. We're not afraid to ask, "What are you doing?" or "How did you do that?" And when you ask those types of questions, they'll tell you. We can't implement every new idea, but when we do hear a good one, we make sure to be receptive. However, there is a difference between adding value to what we've built by finding new and innovative ways to improve our systems and processes and coming in and trying to change how we do things. It's about being able to color within the lines, and when it comes to learning new ways to serve and become more attractive to our customers, we give our employees a lot of leeway, but it has to work within the systems we've created. If you picture our systems and processes like an iPhone, we want someone to come in and show us a bunch of cool new apps we can add to that iPhone, not try to sell us a brand-new iPhone.

There is a flip side to this, and we know that we can't become too comfortable or take a one-size-fits-all approach, so we must walk a fine line. We've learned to never say that we'll never do something again. Things always change, and sometimes we need a fresh, new perspective and someone to shake things up or, in some cases, wake us up to the other possibilities we might not see at the moment. It will always depend on the person and the circumstances, but we need to be open to someone coming in and challenging us. Even then there is a difference between challenging us to improve the process and us telling them what we want them to do and them doing something different. That's disruptive and creates problems with the existing leadership team. It's not good for the future of the company, and most of all it's not good for the customers.

We may utilize science, but we don't always get it right. We've had great success on the technical side, but the leadership and sales positions are the toughest to fill. They are both culture dependent, meaning that you need to espouse the company's values and instill them in those beneath you to succeed in those positions. Over the past twenty years, we've brought in a handful of people for those positions who looked phenomenal on paper; their resume was great, and they appeared to have all the qualifications, but they just weren't the right fit for us. Other times we've broken our own rules and gone against the so-called science. That's something we've regretted almost every single time, and it can lead to disruptive setbacks that we must then figure out how to absorb and correct on the fly. We make mistakes. If you're trying to grow, you will always have those issues, but the key is to learn from those mistakes so you don't make them again.

When looking to fill a leadership position, we've learned that we're much better off with employees with the right cultural fit. That often means promoting proven leaders within our company before trying to recruit superstars from elsewhere. We believe that the people who got us to where we are will be the same people who can get us where we want to go. Besides, we can't just say we value our employees and not take care of them. When they produce, we reward them to keep them motivated, which often means promoting them, but we first want to see them go above and beyond.

Not every lesson we took from our corporate days was negative or informed us what not to do. We both learned early on the importance of advocating for yourself, stepping up, and taking on additional responsibilities. You first have to make sure you're performing and doing a good job with your current assignments. When you grow and prove yourself, the leaders of the company will give you more responsibilities because they want you to be a part of their growth plan. That's a philosophy we share, and it's one we encourage among our own employees. No matter how much success or growth we've experienced over the years, we're most proud of having been able to create a pipeline of talent and watch our team members blossom as professionals. We've hired young people who have excelled, and we made sure to move them up the ranks, even when a position didn't exist beforehand.

Phil Voigt was one of those employees who was always open to the changes we wanted to implement from the beginning. He did everything we needed an engineering director to do without having the title—working with the vendors while managing and maintaining the studio database. Any time we needed to make a change, he was involved, and it was like that for a couple of years. He understood our vision and was 100 percent on board with helping us make that vision a reality. He put in the extra effort, so we created an opportunity for him through a promotion. The position didn't exist before, but we created it for him because we saw that he had talent and a great attitude, and he was already doing the work.

When we gave him a promotion, other employees came to us and said, "I didn't know you were hiring for that position, or I would have applied." We had to say, "Yeah, Phil didn't apply either. We weren't looking for someone to fill that role. Phil stepped up when something needed to be done and demonstrated his leadership. Any one of you could have done the same thing." As Phil continues to step up, perform, and go above and beyond, his role expands as we create additional responsibilities for him. And when other employees see that and know that behavior is rewarded, it creates an incentive within the culture to look for ways to help the company, even if it means going above and beyond what is expected in the current role.

Phil isn't the only one who has stepped up. We're lucky to have several employees who take it upon themselves to do what's necessary to help the organization grow. When we see that occur and can recognize the potential in an employee, we make sure to reward that person. We're always looking for opportunities to help our employees leverage their knowledge and skills to advance their careers. The reality is that this is fun for us. We get so much satisfaction from seeing other people succeed.

And whenever we promote someone, we need to bring new people in underneath them to create the next level of professionals in the organization. We've found that it's often easier to bring in people from outside the industry to fill those positions. As long as they have the right attitude and aptitudes, we're confident that we can teach them our processes and tools. We've had more success with that approach than when trying to bring in someone with industry experience and get them to conform to a culture that might not align with what they're used to. We've had some new employees without industry experience who, in only three to five years, began outperforming veterans with ten to fifteen years of experience.

We believe that this approach reinforces the strong company culture. It's also why we don't have a lot of turnover. We've been fortunate in that regard and take great pride in being able to attract and retain our team members because of our culture. Many of our new team members are referred by our employees, customers, and contractors. We also have a great working relationship with the local unions that provide Alpha with trained and talented employees.

We can talk about how well we pay our employees, the bonuses we provide, and how great the culture is, but it means more coming from them. By far our employees are our biggest advocates and recruiters. There isn't a greater compliment than having people want to come work for you because of the good things they've heard from people inside who are familiar with the company. It also creates its own incentive structure. During a recent interview with a candidate referred to us by an employee, he told us, "I'm going to work twice as hard because I can't let my sister and my brother-in-law down." We never asked for that or expected that, but it's gratifying to hear those words because they reinforce what we set out to create.

Bob Bracken is another employee with a great success story. He was a hard worker who applied himself when we hired him in 2010. His father used to have a photography business. He would take photos for the local sports teams, but when his parents passed away, the business wound down, and Bob was out of a job. He relocated to Milwaukee and gained experience working for an independent control company. That's where he pursued and earned his two-year HVAC degree. He had some experience when he applied, so we took a chance on him, and we're glad we did because he's now our technical team lead in northern Illinois and trains all the young engineers.

A few years later, Bob's wife Sara applied for a part-time position. She didn't land it at first, but when the person we hired for the position left the company, we gave her a shot, and we're glad we did. They are both phenomenal employees committed to the team and helping our customers. Watching our employees and their families thrive makes us realize we're doing right by them.

AN UNLIKELY PATH
By Jason Vogelbaugh: Director of Business Development

I grew up wanting to be a residential carpenter. I wanted to build houses, and I knew that since I was twelve. I didn't plan on going to college because I didn't need to, but I had a drafting teacher in high school who demanded that I apply to at least one university. So after months of his badgering, I applied to the University of Illinois and was accepted into the architectural program. I soon became disillusioned that I wouldn't be Frank Lloyd Wright, so I entered a joint master's program in civil engineering and architecture with a focus on construction management.

As an overeducated carpenter and general contractor, I got a job working with corporate Invensys on a contract for the University of Illinois and was recruited into temperature controls. It was an interesting opportunity with good perks. I had no technical expertise, but they said I didn't need any. Shortly after that, two people reached out to me who were several levels of management above me and asked if I could build a cash-flow model. That turned out to be Frank Rotello and Brent Bernardi. I was still learning about temperature controls, but I did know how to do what they asked, so I built a cash-flow model. We worked together for a short period, and that was it, or so I thought.

Over the next three years, I became involved with bigger and bigger projects, but the company was constantly being restructured, and when I heard they were going to sell the branches, I knew I needed to get out of there. I accepted a job to work with a general contractor out of St. Louis, and I was ready to put my house on the market when my phone rang. It was Frank and Brent. We hadn't spoken in years, but they asked if I would stay with them because they were purchasing two of the branches. I was tired of the corporate politics and restructuring, but they assured me what they were doing was different. I had had a good experience working with them, and they sold me on their pitch. It also beat having to put my home on the market, so I took them up on their offer.

I started working out of their Springfield office and very quickly became the operations manager, not just for Springfield but for the entire company. Meanwhile I watched numerous salespeople come and go, so I wound up in a position where I wrote technical proposals that we presented to customers. I did this while I also oversaw every construction project for the entire company.

I had gone from this guy who didn't know anything about controls to someone who could go out to assess, troubleshoot, and provide solutions to our customers. I was interested in it, and I got pretty good at it, so I decided to start following up. That's when something interesting happened. Contracts and purchase orders started coming in. Customers began asking me for more. So I sold more. In 2008 I sold somewhere around $800,000—$2.4 million in 2009. That's when Frank and Brent said, "You just sold more than what we would have expected for a negotiated salesperson. And you did it while you're also doing the operations manager job. Maybe you should just sell."

I had to look at myself in the mirror and ask, *What am I doing here? I used to be a carpenter who wanted to build houses, but here I am.* It had worked out well so far. I couldn't ask for a better environment or company culture. Frank and Brent had allowed me to grow professionally and as a person, so why not try just selling? What's the worst that could happen? I could always go back to operations.

That's when we traveled to Texas for a training course in energy solutions, and suddenly all my education, training, and experience came together in one moment. That's when the negotiated sales had gone from a hobby within the company to a unique message and offering in temperature controls that Alpha could provide our customers that would give them a return on investment. This was what I knew how to do. That's when the company really took off, and my role in it became so interesting.

48

Alpha is unique in that we develop relationships with mechanical contractors, consulting engineers, and all these other design and construction professionals that we pull into our energy-efficiency projects. What gets me so excited is being able to leverage our partnerships to create these projects that are great for our customers. There are so many examples of customers who were going to spend money on new control systems but were able to take a different approach that would yield a seven-figure project for us while decreasing their annual energy use by 50 percent. It's good for the environment, good for their public image, good for the people working in that building, and good for their shareholders. That's what gets me out of bed in the morning, and I'm always looking for ways to transfer knowledge effectively to other people in the organization, so we can continue to grow.

And to think I was someone who wanted to work in residential construction and knew nothing about temperature controls. I didn't even want to go to college. The fact that I do what I do today is a testament to Frank and Brent's leadership and the culture they've created at Alpha. When you go to work at Alpha, you know that if you do your best, go as hard as possible, and do the right thing, you will be supported. How many companies out there are like that?

IF YOU AREN'T CHANGING, YOU'RE FALLING BEHIND

For a long time, our industry was stable, and people were comfortable doing things the way they had always been done, but that is no longer the case. We work in a highly technical industry, and today the technology and market opportunities constantly change. That requires us to shift gears and change with the landscape so that we don't get left behind or, worse, become unable to satisfy our customers' current needs. If we aren't constantly learning, adjusting, and changing, we're losing ground to the market and the competition. Think about something as routine as bank transactions. When's the last time you went to the actual bank? How many checks do you write these days? The world is a different place than it was only a few years ago, and if we're doing the same thing that we were doing twenty, ten, or even just five years ago, we're probably doing it wrong, and we're almost definitely not doing it as efficiently as possible.

It's one thing to say that we need to evolve, and it's another thing for our employees to grow with us because not every employee has the same attitude toward change. Communication is essential, so everyone understands our reasoning. A tool like the Culture Index is valuable in rooting out some of these issues before they occur, but we've had situations with senior-level people who had a lot of industry knowledge yet were resistant to change. Part of this is just human nature. By no means were any of these employees bad people or unqualified to do their job. They wouldn't have been with us for so long if they weren't talented, but that reluctance to change can put us in a difficult position.

If a more rigid company found itself with individuals reluctant to adapt to the organization's new direction, it might view those employees as expendable. We never do that. We always try to adjust and accommodate employees to allow time for them to move with us, either in their current role or another role the new direction might provide.

Many different situations like this can unexpectedly pop up with employees. Our industry requires our employees to submit to random drug tests, and if someone messes up or makes a poor decision, we must decide if we should give that employee a second or even a third chance. Ultimately that employee must take responsibility for their own life and stop making bad decisions if they want to remain employed at Alpha, but we do have to look out for our people. Sometimes you have to wear different hats as a leader and shift gears to become a person of authority, a friend, or a mentor. You must become that person who is there to give them a nudge in the right direction or a wake-up call when it's necessary. The company might be worse off in the short term, and it might have been easier to move that employee out, but that's not who we are. We have committed to our people, which sometimes requires us to be flexible. Commitment is a two-way street; sometimes we must adapt to a trusted and loyal employee because, in the long run, it will positively impact the culture.

People are people, and no two are alike. The two of us work a lot, and some people are similar to us in that they like to work a lot, but most people today want work to be more efficient. That's why we invest in processes and technologies, so people don't have to work long hours. We don't push them to put in a lot of overtime. We want our employees to have a balanced lifestyle. We strive to provide our employees with flexibility. We've allowed some to work from home if they were in a position that allowed it. We know that when we make things more efficient and the conditions better for our employees, they work harder and are more productive. It's a no-brainer.

Those aren't the only incentives and ways we reward our employees. In addition to contributing to a 401k for our employees, we've created a supplemental profit-sharing program. Different bonus plans are tailor-made for the various positions and contributions to the company. The amount is determined by our company's gross profit. We pay out around 50 percent of our operating profit back to our employees through 401k contributions and bonus plans. That's on top of a good base salary. The way we look at it, if they're helping us grow the business, we want to reward them for their efforts and contributions to the company.

There is no other way to put it: our employees drive our profit. That word has developed a bad connotation lately. Often politicians who have never owned or run a business don't fully understand that profits are necessary to add employees, reinvest in the business, and provide a fair return on investment to the business owners. Not to mention that federal and state taxes are paid from those profits. The reality is that you need to focus on profit when running a business because without it you have nothing. That's why we share that profit with our employees if we have a good year. However, there is another entity that's just as important and without which we would not have a business—the customer. It doesn't matter what your job description is; the organizational structure of our business is designed so we all work for the customer.

CHAPTER 3
START WITH CUSTOMERS

A t Alpha we don't just do the job for the customer, provide a warranty, and consider ourselves done. What's unique about Alpha and companies like us is that our systems, installations, and responsibilities for the customer evolve and continuously have to be updated, maintained, and monitored. That's what makes us different than traditional contractors.

Most of these buildings we service have their own staff to operate and maintain the facilities, so we train those people in our systems and services to help them create the best possible environment. Whether it's a school, government facility, industrial operation, or office building, we try to limit the complaints our customers get from their occupants. On top of that, we help them save energy and maintain the equipment, which extends both the equipment and facility lifespan. That's a return on their investment and a way for them to save money that they can reinvest in what aligns with their own mission.

We work with our customers as a partner over time because we've become part of the operational infrastructure of their facilities. If we viewed the relationship with our customers as purely transactional, we could never build the organization we needed to be successful. We have to look at our relationships with our customers like a marriage.

We're committed to each other, which means that we need to be fair to that customer and remain a trusted advisor if we're going to continue that relationship for years or decades to come. And if we're not serving as that trusted advisor to our customers, we're not doing our job. We're very sensitive to that, so we always challenge ourselves to determine what the customer needs and how we can improve upon delivering that need. Like our staff is comprised of a wide array of different personalities, so are our customers. Our goal remains to not only serve them and meet their expectations, but also to exceed them both on the product and aftermarket service sides.

Customers might be happy and comfortable with what's working now, but markets fluctuate, and technology changes. Through it all we must provide solutions to help our customers navigate that changing landscape, whether they see it coming or not. Change is inevitable. It's going to happen; we must prepare the customer so they're ready for it. That requires staying one step ahead and continually asking ourselves how we can help our customers run their facilities more efficiently and effectively while saving energy and creating a safer environment. It's never about where we are today. It's about how we get to where we need to go. We always try to think of the bigger picture by looking ahead to the future. That might require looking at other market areas and seeing what technology we can implement. Finding that unique solution for our customers drives everything we do, but this is often easier said than done.

Just like with some employees who are set in their ways and comfortable with how things are, the same is true about some of our customers. Reluctance to change is human nature. Customers may not understand a new process or technology, which can create discomfort. That's why it's absolutely imperative that all of our employees are on board with the direction we're going and what we want to do because our messaging must be consistent when we approach the customer so they understand what we're trying to do and why.

We don't look at it like we're selling something to our customers because that isn't accurate. It's more that we're trying to solve (or avoid) a problem and provide them with a solution. That's how we present it, and we're constantly trying to get that messaging right. So when we start a new energy project, we try to meet not only with the facility director, but also with all the key leaders in that facility, so they understand what we're doing and how that will create a more comfortable, secure, and energy-efficient facility. That way, everyone is on board, and they understand not only how we do things, but also why we do things. That allows us to better work with the customer's team to create a good working relationship for the long term, so when there comes a time down the road when we need to implement a new process or technology, we have already established those open lines of communication. And with issues like cybersecurity becoming more prevalent every year, we need to update these systems more frequently than ever before.

Sometimes the opposite is also true, and a particular customer might want us to do things a certain way or take a different approach that might provide a different solution. Today customers can hear lots of things about what's possible and what they could be doing instead, but not all of it is practical. We attended the Realcomm IBcon conferences years ago that discussed smart building technologies that still haven't come to fruition in our market area, so not everything being discussed is a practical solution or even right for that customer.

This is why our primary job is to serve as that trusted advisor for our customers to help them navigate the landscape and cut through the noise. Given how quickly technology changes our industry, we must have complex conversations with our customers. And when they ask for something that we aren't already providing or recommending, we first must figure out if that's a practical request. If it is, then that's what we work to do, but if it's not, we must tell the customer we understand them and wish we could help them, but what they want can't happen because of cost or budget constraints. It might be something out of our control or something we would have to work out with the manufacturer. If that remains a sticking point, we sometimes must reconsider if we should do business with that customer.

Not every customer is meant to be your customer. It doesn't matter what you do and who you are; that's just the reality of doing business.

> ## Not every customer is meant to be your customer.

Even if you don't sever a relationship with a customer, sometimes you just grow apart or just don't grow together. We've worked with customers on successful projects and had good working relationships, but they didn't blossom for whatever reason. Nothing went wrong, and there weren't any issues, but the seed we planted didn't produce any fruit. Those relationships are few and far between, but they do happen.

WE MUST BE FAIR TO THE CUSTOMERS

Whether attracting new customers or maintaining healthy relationships with existing customers, we must look beyond our needs to ensure we're being fair to the customers. Sometimes that can be a balancing act. When we tried to venture into the mechanical services business in central and northern Illinois, we became so focused on growing and implementing new solutions that when we peeled back the onion, we realized that we were actually losing money for the first time in that area of the business. In our attempt to be fair to our customers, we went too far, so we brought the entire team together for a meeting to remind everyone that we also had to be fair to Alpha. Every customer may be different, but over the years we've established a set of guidelines that help ensure that our employees are always being fair to the customer and, in turn, to Alpha.

#1. ADMIT WHEN YOU DON'T KNOW THE ANSWER

When Alpha first started, we worked with one of the most technically knowledgeable customers we've ever had, even going back to our corporate days, and we had worked with manufacturers and technology companies all over the globe. In this case the customer had researchers who had spent time understanding the technology, so they knew more about the systems than our team members. They ended up testing our team members' aptitude and knowledge by asking them questions they would have no way of knowing the answers to. Instead of simply admitting that they didn't know the answers, our team members made the mistake of guessing the answer. And, of course, they guessed wrong. That immediately killed our credibility.

The reality is that if you are 99 percent sure, then you really don't know the answer. You are either 100 percent sure, or you don't know. You must have the guts to admit that you don't know something because if you guess wrong, you can not only kill your credibility, but also risk making a mistake. That type of disruption can cost time and money. Nobody knows everything, so whenever our team members don't have the answer to a customer's question, they tell the customer they will find out and come back with the answer. The secondary value of this approach is that you have a valid reason to speak with your customer again.

#2. KEEP LINES OF COMMUNICATION OPEN

Communication is a two-way street. That channel is important for conveying your needs and explaining what you're trying to accomplish and why, but you also need to listen to the customer's needs. Too many people forget that second part, but there is listening, and then there is active listening. We encourage active listening by our team members so they have a better chance of understanding not only what the customer needs, but also why.

When we had issues with a very good but demanding customer, we set up quarterly meetings to discuss those issues. That opened up those lines of communication. You can't solve problems without communication. That builds trust and allows you to stop pointing fingers and taking things personally and start getting to the heart of the real issue. We knew that we had to adapt, but we also knew that we needed to rebuild the trust that had deteriorated, so we did that through a series of smaller pilot jobs when it came time to upgrade our technology.

Not only did this approach improve our working relationship with the customer, but it also opened up the lines of communication within our company. That allowed us to reevaluate our processes and learn more about our team. The relationship with that customer was challenging and frustrating when it was happening, but in hindsight it was really a major success because it allowed us to improve our processes, which benefited all of our customers.

We still hold those meetings with that customer to keep that dialogue open so both organizations will continue to benefit, but there are far fewer complaints. We now spend only a few minutes (if any at all) on project problems and use the rest of the time to have proactive discussions on how they can deploy our technologies to make their building more comfortable, secure, and efficient. It's been quite an evolution.

#3. ADDRESS THE PROBLEM IMMEDIATELY

We saw countless examples of this in the corporate world where people wouldn't address a problem, try to sweep it under the rug, or just pretend it didn't exist because they didn't want to get in trouble or have to take responsibility. Just because the customer isn't aware of the problem doesn't mean that there isn't a problem. Eventually, without fail, those problems came to light, but by that point the customer was so furious that we had to spend twice as much to fix the problem and keep them happy. In some cases we were lucky to keep them at all. Not only did this cost more money, but also addressing the problem required pulling resources from other areas of the company, so there was a ripple effect. Add to that the time it takes to reestablish trust with the customer, and it's just not worth it. The solution is simple: we bite the bullet when we see a problem. You can't battle that. You have to find a fair and equitable solution for the customer because you not only want to keep the customer happy, but you also want to keep the customer.

We made a very costly mistake with one of our first big clients. When it surfaced, the customer expected a fight, but we didn't give them one. We didn't try to B.S. our way around the issue; we just fixed it. Our project team took responsibility and worked extra hours without pay to resolve the problem. That was something the customer must have appreciated because that action was the first step in building a long-term customer relationship. It proved to be a win-win for everyone and taught us a valuable lesson.

All kinds of things can (and will) go wrong in any business, but what's important is how you respond, both internally with your employees and externally with your customers. If you deal with it fairly, that can be the difference between keeping and losing that customer. You always want to be thinking long term and be cognizant of how short-term actions influence that relationship and keep you on track.

#4. FOCUS ON THE SMALL THINGS

There was a company president we worked with for a short time who used to say, "If you take care of the bits, the big things will take care of themselves." It's such a simple yet powerful statement because the big things are nothing but a conglomeration of the bits or the little things.

If you go into a round of golf determined to break eighty and focus only on breaking eighty, not each individual shot, you're never going to accomplish your goal. The only shot that matters in golf is the next one, and each one is its own universe that requires all your attention and effort. Only once you approach the game like that can you achieve the bigger overall goal of breaking eighty. It's the same thing in business. Focus on the little things, and the big things will take care of themselves.

ALL EYES ON THE CUSTOMER

CUSTOMER

Business Development

Project Management

Design & Controls Engineering

Service & Construction Management

Owners

Business Operations

Electrical Installation

Mechanical Service & Installation

THE ORGANIZATION IS BIGGER THAN JUST ONE PERSON

When we worked at corporate, most branches assigned one employee to serve a customer to ensure everything was consistent at that facility. We didn't send anyone else to work on that project because they might do it differently—not better or worse, just their own way. But what happens if that person goes away on vacation or gets sick? What if that customer has needs beyond what that person can fulfill?

Even when the customer liked the employee and thought they were doing a great job, the closer we looked, we realized that was not always the case. That personal connection is still critical, but individuals can deviate from the structure and hide many things. However, when you have standards, documented processes, and procedures, your employees become part of a team with quality control measures in place. Everything is documented, so we know it's all being done the same way and the right way every single time. By doing that, you effectively multiply yourself, your individual employees, and the organization.

When we oversaw all of the branches at Invensys, we saw several that worked together as a team to serve the customer, and they were highly successful doing it, but it was difficult, if not impossible, to make all of the branch managers see it that way. So when we started Alpha, we knew that having a customer dependent on one person was no way to run a ship. We wanted the entire organization to serve the customer, not one individual. To us it wasn't a risk because we had seen the models to prove that it would grow a profitable business while adding value to our customers. However, the customer didn't always see it that way, so we often had conversations to reset their expectations. Some of them were stuck in their ways and had grown so used to that one individual they had worked with that it took some time to gain their confidence in the Alpha Team approach. We'd often hear things like, "The only guy I want to serve my site is Jeff. He's the reason I love Alpha."

We made sure to tell them, "Thank you! We're grateful for Jeff, but we can't do that. We have several quality people like Jeff who have great ideas, but those ideas aren't exclusive to those individuals. We gather them all up, and they become Alpha's ideas. So you'll have the best of Alpha serving you and adding more value to your business than any one person ever could."

We want the solution provided by Alpha to look exactly the same no matter who delivers it, and we want that deliverable to be as consistent as if it were coming off a production line, so they couldn't tell who on our team worked on their project. That unified approach is important because when Alpha works with a customer, we are only one part of what is sometimes a large team of construction professionals needed to make that project a success. We must work on the plans and specifications with other contractors and subcontractors. When a problem arises, rarely are individuals willing to accept blame or take responsibility. That leads to a lot of finger-pointing and a frustrated customer. In those situations everyone owns a little piece of the problem and the solution. It requires quickly coming to a consensus to create the best possible outcome for the customer.

> *We want the solution provided by Alpha to look exactly the same no matter who delivers it.*

Similar to how we don't want only one of our employees to be the face of Alpha for a particular customer, it does us no good when the roles are reversed, and we're the ones who have a relationship with only one person within the organization we're working with. Organizations change people all the time, and if that one person leaves or changes roles within the company, our relationship with that customer is at risk. Expanding our relationship within our customers' organization lets us remain connected with their needs and our solution offerings for an extended period.

Many of our customers once had the benefit of knowledgeable people who came up in the industry. They continued to learn, so they had decades of experience managing their facility, but experts like that are few and far between on the corporate side today. What's happening is that many of these people with that particular experience are retiring or leaving the business. In some cases the company chooses not to fill those positions, and middle management is essentially gone because the company can leverage technology instead. In other cases those people with specific experience are replaced by those with much more generic experience. They may know about project management and employee supervision but don't know the ins and outs of our industry like their predecessors because technology has allowed their facilities to run independently, so there is no need to acquire that knowledge. As a result they might not be managing or utilizing our technology properly, and they typically don't have the best understanding of their systems and utility costs. The burden falls on us to make sure we're at the table with them, educating them as we continue to modernize, so we can help them get the maximum return on their investment.

This trend has been exacerbated by COVID. Before the pandemic some of these veterans who were close to retirement felt stuck on the hamster wheel and didn't think they could quit. They were doing what they had done their entire lives and didn't want to do anything else, but when life was disrupted the way it was during 2020, they realized they didn't have to work every day of their lives and made a change.

We noticed these shifts in employee experience occur in our industry over the past few decades, but it's also happening in others. We can see it with some of our customers, and the trend is growing. And given the significant focus on quarterly performance in the past forty-five years, there is about a nine- to twelve-month internal commitment to a position in Corporate America. That person won't necessarily leave the company after that time, but they will often change roles. That means that the decisions and actions the original person put in motion continue to influence their sphere after they've left, but they never have to live with the consequences, good or bad, of those decisions they made. Those people then move on to their next position and tend to do things the exact same way without ever being able to see the fruits of their previous efforts. They don't even know if they won or lost most of the time. When you don't know the result, it's easy to convince yourself that it's the right way to do things because that's how you did it last time. You keep playing the same game over and over again but have no way of knowing if you're on the right path.

> One of our biggest challenges today is being able to communicate to our customers what their own needs even are.

Because of all of these changes, one of our biggest challenges today is being able to communicate to our customers what their own needs even are. In the past we spoke the same language. Now we have to be much more specific and provide more background just to get on the same page. That wasn't the case as few as five years ago, but today it often feels like we're starting from scratch regarding our communication.

We can't control what they do in Corporate America or how our customers choose to run their business. We can only control what we do, and we understand that the benefit of the approach we take at Alpha as business owners is that we are there and can see the impact of our decisions and our team members' decisions. If there is something we can do better, we learn from that and adjust. That's one of the biggest differences between Corporate America and private business ownership these days.

LOOKING AHEAD

We know that we can't work with everyone we want to, but Alpha is fortunate to be in a position where we can be more selective in who we take on as customers. Similar to how we rely on a tool like the Culture Index to prequalify our employees to make sure they're a good fit, we need to do something similar to vet our customers to see if we'd be a good fit for them and what they want to do before pursuing a specific job. It's essential that we do our own homework by prequalifying our customers because some just aren't ready to make those changes.

It helps to have a champion within the customer's company who understands our vision and what we're trying to do, or else we'll be fighting an uphill battle. If we push a customer too hard and that customer is not ready or committed, we probably won't have much success, so there is a fine line we must walk. Those internal champions on the customer's team are crucial because they are often the ones going to the board for approval or the ones with the responsibility of allocating taxpayer money. We must ensure they understand what we're capable of and why we're implementing certain changes.

The challenge is how we demonstrate our value, and we want customers to see us as an innovative company that can bring leading-edge technology and work with them to deploy it effectively—a company that can create a safe and comfortable environment in their facility with good air quality while still being energy efficient. We want them to know that they will have fewer issues when Alpha is on the job and working as part of the contracting team. In nine out of ten cases, we do not position our offerings based on price. We focus on value, so our customers realize that Alpha delivers a higher value because there is less management and supervision required by the customer during normal operations. The biggest win for customers is that they can be assured of a positive return on their investment. What's most important is that any potential customers view us as a true partner.

That's the reputation we've worked hard to build over the past twenty years, and we hope that it makes us appear less of a risk to hire compared to our competitors. And as we've grown bigger, more competitors have come knocking on our customers' doors. We pay attention to what our competitors are doing, and we're conscious of their influences on our marketplace, but we strive to remain on our own course and execute what we believe we need to do to succeed.

Someone once told us that if you believe what you're doing is right and your team is taking the right action, then every customer deserves the opportunity to work with you. That stuck with us. It's hard to argue with it.

CHAPTER 4
CREATING EFFICIENT SYSTEMS, PROCESSES, AND STANDARDS

After years of witnessing the effort corporate put into maintaining certain procedures that never added any value, we focused only on the critical things when we started Alpha. The Rockford and Springfield branches may have come with active projects and customer relationships when we took them over, but they didn't come with the necessary support structure we wanted. Suddenly we were responsible for all the facilities and the employees who managed those facilities, so before we did anything else, we looked at the company's critical functions and tried to create a series of efficient standards and processes around those functions.

We had to meet the needs of our employees before we could expect them to meet the needs of our customers, sustain our backlog of projects, and allow room for new bookings to grow our

> Before we did anything else, we looked at the company's critical functions and tried to create a series of efficient standards and processes around those functions.

business. There were a lot of questions we needed to answer. *How do we uphold our responsibility to our employees? How can we give them the support they need so they feel comfortable? What services will we provide? How do we give them all the information and data they need, so they can properly do their job?*

There were two types of processes we needed to create: internal (operations and administration) and external (customer facing). The foundation and structure of the company had to be in place before we could even think about executing a project, so we started with internal processes.

The two of us made a list of every function we needed to put in place, and we split the responsibility down the middle. In the beginning we designed our org chart to be as flat as possible; everyone reported directly to one of the two of us. There were no additional layers, so we were responsible for driving change. We knew that as the company grew, so would the structure, but from the beginning it was crucial to ensure that structure never became too complex. We strived to remain lean, but without compromising the product or service we provided, so we created better benefit offerings for our salaried staff, HR solutions, and proper payroll and tax filings.

We were fortunate to have former team members want to join us at Alpha. They brought with them key knowledge and skills they had learned while at the corporation with us. As we began the process of initializing the Alpha operations, Vickie and Susan leveraged their industry knowledge and expertise to help us set up our ERP (financial and business operations software), establish business operations processes, and train the team members. Vickie was responsible for contract administration, accounts receivable, and salaried and union payrolls. Susan was responsible for purchasing, inventory, and accounts payable. She also became the Alpha ERP "Jonas" expert for configuring and maintaining all of the various financial and business operations modules. As the business continued to grow, Vickie and Susan helped train new members of the business operations support team. Their dedication to Alpha and commitment to our customers is another example of how individual efforts and working in a team environment contribute to Alpha's success.

With our infrastructure in place, we could focus on the external processes. Our customers needed to know that they were getting a consistent product when they hired Alpha. That's achieved by implementing a standardization and documentation process throughout the organization. If we did it right once, we could do it right a thousand times, and if someone on the team had to step away, someone else could step in and do the job the same exact way as the person before. But if anyone on our team veered off course or decided to forge a separate path, we would no longer have consistent standards and processes, which would make it difficult to grow. When trying to put these processes in place, it's easy to get bogged down in formalities and policy procedure documents, so we made it a point not to micromanage.

Creating efficient processes is essential because we don't do any of this alone. Alpha works with various subcontractors during different project phases, the most significant being our partnership with Schneider Electric. They provide all the products and technologies we deploy, but they aren't our only partners. Whether it's our relationship with banking and insurance entities or electrical/mechanical subcontractors, each is an essential partner that helps us maintain both our internal and external systems and processes. We need to have healthy working relationships with all our partners, so we can work together to bring projects in on time and on budget. The entire ecosystem needs to be in sync because every piece fits together. That is the ultimate goal, no matter who we work with or work for.

We're juggling a lot, and all the pieces are constantly in motion. Teams are given responsibilities, and the team leaders are in place to hold them accountable. Multiple people work with multiple teams on multiple projects. There are different start dates, finish dates, and various complexities along the way, which make resource allocation and scheduling critical. No matter where our customers are located, all of our people must do their job the same way on a daily, weekly, monthly, and yearly basis. To keep track of all that, we need efficient processes. We inherited some of those from corporate, so they were already in place when we started. Others we enhanced, and some we replaced or eliminated.

No matter where it originated or how it evolved, we set out to make each one as transparent, visible, and accessible as possible to those who operated within our ecosystem. Still, it can be difficult to get everyone on the same page, especially if the team member has been with the previous company. Paradigm shifts are a challenge for all of us. It takes time, repetition, and consistency to create lasting change. For new employees it's much easier if the team member has joined the organization with the intent of becoming part of the ecosystem and learning the standards and process. This ties directly back to the hiring criteria for new team members.

A PROCESS IS ONLY AS VALUABLE AS THE PEOPLE IMPLEMENTING IT

It's challenging to run a multicity and multidisciplined organization when the branches don't all adhere to a consistent standard, but that's precisely what was happening when we took over the Rockford and Springfield branches.

The branches and their managers were autonomous, which basically meant they did things the way they wanted. At first we kept an administrative person in each of the two offices because the managers felt that was the only way they could function, but after a year or two, we discovered that the administrative person was creating their own structures and processes. When you leave things for people to do their own way, you get inconsistencies, but that wasn't the only pushback we encountered.

During the early years of Alpha, we experienced resistance to the changes we wanted to implement in just about every section of the business, but none of this was new. It was expected, because we dealt with this firsthand back at corporate. Whenever we tried to implement something new, a third of the employees were on board, a third were neutral, and a third fought us the entire way. They either believed they were smarter, insisted on doing things their own way, or just rejected it outright because they weren't going to bend to "corporate puke." We

> *Whenever we tried to implement something new, a third of the employees were on board, a third were neutral, and a third fought us the entire way.*

heard every excuse in the book. "This is stupid." "This is hard." "We don't want to do it this way." "This is going to break the company."

We had a vision for Alpha and a system that we believed would be transformational for our customers, but that didn't mean anything if we didn't have the entire team on board ready to execute. Some veteran managers who had been with the company since the corporate days were the most resistant to change. These were people who had been in charge, so they felt the way they managed their people was best for the company. What we wanted to do was so far out of their comfort zone that it was foreign. Whether they didn't want to put in the extra work or just weren't interested in learning anything new, they fought us and desperately wanted to keep doing things the old way. And when the leadership team isn't on board with the mother ship, it creates inconsistencies across the board.

It wasn't just management. Some members of the design team also put up a fight because they didn't want standards. They wanted to do things their way. They thought of themselves as artists—technical artists—and you aren't going to tell technical artists that they need to do things the exact same way every time. They wanted their process and the result to be unique to them. Because of that thinking, the standardization of the design team slowly dissolved over time. It didn't go over well when we came in and told them we wanted everyone to start doing things the same way. Some of them were on board with our vision, but other folks had been doing things their way for so long (decades in some cases) that it felt unnatural, and they took it personally. They looked at all the new variables we were trying to impose as risky, and true designers are risk averse because they must make sure they don't make mistakes. There was no getting some of those folks to do things any other way. That created negative energy, which led to inefficiency, missed opportunities, and decreased profit. Worst of all, it was doing a disservice to our customers.

We were in a bind and had a choice to make: either cut ties with everyone who didn't align with our vision, or have patience and allow these changes to develop over time. We chose the latter, even if it meant our vision for Alpha wouldn't be initially realized. Sure, we could have been hell-bent on making these changes and replaced those loyal veterans who weren't on board, but that would mean our vision was more important than our team members. That wasn't the case. So when we encountered resistance, we compromised and adapted. We would never abandon our vision or values, but we don't abandon our employees either because that wouldn't be fair, and everything we do must come down to fairness. That's a value we can't ever compromise on. We still had to take care of the business, but we had the patience to say, "Hold on. Let's figure this out together."

Patience is a quality that's often overlooked and undervalued by many leaders because you can't control everything, and you certainly can't control people. People are unpredictable. Sometimes they say they will do one thing and end up doing another. That's a given, so patience is something we've always prioritized, and some of our team members have even pointed it out after the fact. But practicing patience can be exhausting. A fine line needs to be walked because it's possible to have too much patience and give someone the benefit of the doubt for too long. Even our patience runs out, and when our first ten years at Alpha weren't as profitable as expected, we inevitably reached a point where we felt we had to pull the trigger and say, "We need to make a change."

As some of our veteran managers retired, employees approached us to say, "I'd like to be considered for that position now that it's open," and we'd tell them, "Unfortunately, that position retired with that person. It doesn't exist anymore."

It may sound harsh, but that was the only way we could get people to pay attention and understand that we were serious about not doing things the old way anymore. We can preach all day long about what we believe the best practices to be, but if the employees don't believe in it or accept it, the culture won't change, and neither will the company. Leaders who are on board with our vision drive those changes down through the entire organization. It doesn't matter what we're trying to do—everything from providing our employees with the necessary information, remaining in compliance, updating payroll, and improving HR—it's impossible for it to be effective if the leaders don't share our vision. It's true on the administrative side and the operations side.

That's why getting the right person for the right job is crucial. This doesn't mean that they must be young or impressionable. We've had experienced people who had left the corporate world but weren't yet ready to retire approach us about job opportunities because they heard of the way we do things at Alpha. They don't know us by name, just Alpha by reputation, and that was the ultimate compliment to us. They appreciate the structure, so they do a phenomenal job when we bring them in. Some of those who had worked for our competitors tell us how much they appreciate the leadership at Alpha and how it's night and day compared to their previous position. That reinforces the importance of creating a solid company culture and reminds us that we have been on the right track.

New people can bring a unique perspective, and one of those people for us was Wendy. We hired Wendy to manage the dispatching and scheduling for our service group in 2014. She was another long-term Invensys employee who was looking for a change when she decided to join the Alpha team. Wendy has since taken this role to a whole new level. She keeps track of all the work orders and constantly communicates with the various offices across two states to ensure that our team members can satisfy the customer. She knows exactly what's going on, and when she doesn't she makes sure to find out. She's a bulldog who consistently follows up and gets answers. You don't mess with Wendy! With her at the helm, we're confident that everyone knows their responsibility to the team and the customer. That takes a lot off our minds because we can't be on top of every little thing. The machine needs to run without our input. We set it in motion, let our people do their thing, and get out of the way.

Wendy is the epitome of having the right person in the right job, and when other employees can see the value that a new way of doing things adds to the company, they develop a new appreciation for that system. Even many of those who fought us in the beginning came around when they understood the benefit. It's all part of the maturation process, but it must start with the employees, and it will almost always require patience.

That relationship with our employees is a two-way street. It's not all about what they do for us; it's also about how we care for them and reward them when they go above and beyond. Whether it's something small like a gift card, or a much bigger discretionary bonus, we make it a point to recognize good work because that transforms the company. When they add value, we also make sure they rise in the organization. We need our employees to understand that their contribution matters, and rewards

> *The machine needs to run without our input. We set it in motion, let our people do their thing, and get out of the way.*

help tie a bow on things while keeping everyone happy, on board, and moving in the same direction. When that happens, the improvement within the organization is immeasurable because we can focus on rooting out problems and improving those systems. And there is always room for improvement.

A TEAM EFFORT
By Phil Voigt: Director of Engineering Solutions

When you get five engineers in the room, you'll get five different opinions, and each one of those engineers will want to prove they are the smartest. It might have a little to do with human nature, but engineers, in particular, are very protective of their work and intellectual property. It's part of their identity, but it leads to a general lack of teamwork.

I've always been annoyed with the inefficiencies created due to people being lone wolves. That's why when I came on board at Alpha in 2007, it was so refreshing to see Frank and Brent encouraging standardization. They always stood behind me when I tried to get people to talk to each other and share everything from drawings, schedules, and tools that helped them complete their various tasks. I always tried to lead by example and ask questions. "Hey guys, how do you do that?"

That all sounds great on paper, but not everyone was on board at first. Many of those early efforts to standardize our process were met with pushback. I once had an engineer tell me, "I'm gonna work myself out of a job if I help you do this." I'd also hear things like, "I've always done things this way; why should I change now?" or "Do you want me to turn off my brain and become a robot?" Engineers can get into such specific details that they'll have discussions on which font to use, but it's that attention to detail that makes them good at what they do.

I understand the instinct to push back against standardization. When people have found a way that works for them and have done it for a long time, they're less open to change, but I have to assure them that we're not trying to stifle their creativity. It's about helping the company by increasing our efficiency as a team. When you think of it like that, who cares who the smartest one in the group is or who has the best idea? You can be a great engineer, but the company is losing if you aren't sharing what you've learned and what you know with the rest of the team. That's how we can be more productive as a whole. We want our people to use their brains—it's why they're with us—but if we can standardize the grunt work or the low-hanging fruit, we can let them flex their muscles when it comes to the more challenging and more important stuff. So instead of starting from scratch every single time, why not piggyback on what we've done in the past that works?

We tried to help our people understand the purpose and why we do what we do, but if that didn't work, sometimes the best way to get them on board was simply by proving them wrong. That's a blunt way of phrasing it, but nothing sinks in quite like seeing the error of your own ways. That's when you can walk them through it and explain why we do things the way we do. If they can see how certain standards would have made things easier or helped them get it right the first time, it clicks, and their attitude changes. We as leaders also have to be patient. It involves compromise on our part and sometimes even turning to the team to help create the process, so they know they are being heard.

One great example of how standardization has improved what we do is our takeoff to proposal process (T2P). This takes the big overall job of an engineer and breaks it down into smaller steps. This way we can take someone who doesn't have much industry experience and start them off with some basic, bite-sized tasks. It prevents them from getting in over their head while letting them still be productive. They can then learn from those more experienced people how what they're doing matters and fits into the bigger overall process. They're learning on the job, which helps them become productive very fast while getting them more familiar with the industry.

It took us a while to find the right people, get them trained, and get them on board with our vision. Culture Index helped a lot with that, and it's also a credit to Frank and Brent for creating an atmosphere that allows these changes to occur. I'm now watching it all come together before my eyes, and I feel like our team has reached a point where we're cruising along. We're seeing the fruit of that hard work we've been investing over the past few years, and there is nothing I enjoy more than seeing people on my team succeed.

We no longer have any lone wolves on our team. If one person on the team has a great idea, they share it with everyone. This is true of mistakes, too, because when one of us learns something the hard way, we all benefit. That information moves us forward and prevents us from having to reinvent the wheel over and over again. Now that we've hit our stride, I'm really looking forward to seeing where this is going and what this team can accomplish.

A NEW WAY TO DO THINGS

We book between 250 and 300 new projects each year, and they range from $5,000 up to $2 million. The service business that provides maintenance and upkeep of our equipment is entirely different and often fulfilled by a different set of technicians explicitly dedicated to service. That business is operational in two states, and we get over five thousand work orders a year. Things move so quickly in the service business, but there is an inherent lack of structure because much of service is about reacting. You're responding to a condition or a problem that might not have existed moments earlier. It's like getting a flat tire. You never plan for that, but you must deal with it, and how you deal with it depends on the situation. Can you patch it up? Do you need to replace the tire? There are so many different variables that you must react to, and that can create issues for a transaction-oriented business, but we must find a way to stay on top of it all.

In the beginning our service business came over with the branches, so we inherited their processes with it as well. We'd get a call from a customer about some equipment and send one of our people over with a clipboard filled with blank forms, so they had to write everything down manually. Remember that these are pipefitters and electricians—guys who work with their hands—so paperwork was not their strong suit.

Getting started with any service project was difficult, but so was closing it out. That became the source of much dissatisfaction and wasted time. When our people finished, they were quickly off to the next job, so the paperwork wasn't being filed on time. It would often take a week, two, or sometimes even a month for customers to receive their invoices. Our employees sometimes waited so long to complete their paperwork that they couldn't remember the services they provided.

That meant digging back through their records and talking to team members to figure out what to bill for. Sometimes it wasn't accurate, and customers questioned the items on the invoice. Since nobody could remember exactly what was done, we'd eliminate or miss some of the items, and that's inefficient waste that can cost us money. Other times the customer would forget about a work order because, after the service was completed that we were invoicing for, we might have done two or three more things, so they were confused. They don't remember what needed to be done and when they asked us to do it.

We consider our technicians best-in-class craftsmen. That means cleaning up after themselves and leaving the job site in a better condition than how they found it. And when you're in the service business, part of your cleanup is your documentation. We instilled in our employees that a job was not finished until it was documented, and the work order was submitted at the end of the day.

If we wanted to be more efficient and stay on top of it all, there needed to be a system in place. In our personal lives, we're used to making a transaction and getting an invoice. That's what we wanted to replicate, so the professional experience for our customers better resembled the invoice process they had grown used to in their daily lives.

Everything came together in 2003 with the implementation of Jonas, our new enterprise resource planning (ERP) system that efficiently organized all our modules. This system was valuable because it allowed us to better document all our work and provide the proper support to cross-train new employees. We kept improving, updating, and streamlining the process to eliminate the extra steps. We received feedback from our customers and even took a look at what our competitors were doing, put it all together, and finally arrived at the completely paperless system we have today. That's something that sets us apart from our competition.

Whether looking up a big new project or a service work order, all our people had access to the same information all in one place, no matter where they were. Everyone became aware of their individual responsibilities, and they could also see what everyone else on their team needed to do, when it needed to be done, and who was responsible for backup if something went wrong. The worst thing that could happen was someone working on a project got pulled away or went on vacation, and the work stopped because the next person wasn't properly trained. This system was our one-stop shop for how we tracked progress, organized transactions, completed the process of billing, and measured our overall performance. This was where Wendy stepped up and added value to the service business. She helps things run smoothly, and now that she has all the essential data she needs at her fingertips, she can troubleshoot whenever there is a blip on the radar. She has such a good grasp of what's going on and a knack for working with people in the field, so nothing falls through the cracks.

We also had to think about the long game. This ERP had to be properly set up, so there wouldn't be problems down the road. We've seen other businesses make that mistake and then try to convert to a new system, but that's not a model for success. Our ERP was scalable. We were able to build on it, so it has grown over time and continues to grow as we add new people and get ready for the next levels of growth. You need systems and practices in place when you have three hundred new projects and five thousand service orders across two states and four offices. Jonas was a big piece of that

> *Our goal today is to get that invoice into our customers' hands within twenty-four hours of completed work.*

puzzle. Gone are the days when we couldn't get our people in the field to close out projects.

We became so efficient that we started selecting our vendors based on their ability to email us invoices on the day our team purchased parts required for service. This became critical for the service side of the business to run smoothly and keep our people continually looking forward instead of having to stop and sift through their records to create a receipt for a task they performed days earlier.

Our goal today is to get that invoice into our customers' hands within twenty-four hours of completed work. Sure, we could have told our employees to complete all their work orders and paperwork by the end of the week on Friday, but what would often happen is that they planned on taking care of everything on Friday afternoon, so paperwork piled up all week. Something would inevitably come up Friday that would push this paperwork until Monday, and suddenly we're a week behind. Then it's the same old thing all over again, and employees are left trying to remember the work they did on that project while the rest of the team is sitting around and waiting. By making this a daily requirement, there is no escape, and only when all the paperwork is filed and the invoice is sent will the project be complete.

That's common sense, and it sounds like it should be easy to execute, but it requires a lot of work and discipline. When we'd bring it up, our people would say, "Yeah, yeah, yeah," but it wouldn't always get done. Some made it sound like we were asking them to cut off their right arm, but we dug in and made it a requirement. And we didn't stop with invoicing. We created a new company-wide set of standards and processes. We printed them out for every new employee during the onboarding process—we even laminated them. They read,

I pledge to…

❑ Not roll to a job without a work order or project number (ever).

❑ Know the scope of my service or project work before beginning any tasks.

❑ Know how many hours have been estimated for engineering, installation, programming, graphics, check out, and commissioning.

❑ Raise my hand early if I feel I cannot complete within the estimated hours.

❑ Communicate timely and openly with the team leader, admin team, or work order as to status and possible issues.

❑ Not perform work outside of scope without prior approval.

❑ Raise technical issues to my supervisor or team leader to promptly avoid wasted troubleshooting time on projects or work orders.

❑ Follow the communications flow internally and not jump the line of communications.

❑ Utilize Outlook email, tasks, and calendars to improve planning and organization skills, providing a basis for weekly updates and better team communicators.

❑ Accurately fill out my timesheet daily and on time.

❑ Complete my work order ticket using E-mobile before I leave the customer's site.

❑ Complete my weekly project update.

❑ Use the "rolling issues log" on every project.

❑ Follow the project closeout process.

We made sure to hammer this policy into the heads of our employees, and we did that through repetition because it's human nature not to change the way you do things until you hear it reinforced multiple times. The first few times it might not register, or you might not think it will catch on, but by the third or fourth time, you understand that it's here to stay and it's important, so you better learn it.

This was not intended to make anyone's life miserable. These are necessary steps in the process so the next person can do their job, and the whole machine can run smoothly. These steps ensure that our technicians understand the scope of each job and have all the necessary information before arriving. If they don't, or there is a disconnect, they must make that clear as early as possible. Much of this process comes down to communication and utilizing the tools at our disposal, so we can intervene and troubleshoot any issues as soon as they arise. These jobs can get complex, and we don't want our people wasting time spinning their wheels. It's like the difference between keeping score or not when playing golf. When you keep score, you have a much better idea where you can improve because you pay closer attention, but if you aren't keeping score, it's harder to grasp where you stand. It's a completely different game.

Because of the systems and processes now in place, this way of working has become so ingrained in how we do things today and how we work together as a team that we rarely have to discuss these points anymore. They have become standard practice. In the corporate days, we used to have what was called the "problem job list" that would be sent out to all the branches, and senior management spent an entire day going through that list item by item. We no longer have a problem job list because we've put the systems in place to deal with problems promptly and proactively as they arise.

This became the basis for the productivity and enhancement workshops for the execution teams. Just doing these straightforward, common-sense things makes everyone's job much easier. It improves our ability to work efficiently as a team, which improves how we serve our customers and increases our profit. If you look closely at what makes a successful organization run smoothly, it almost always comes down to efficient standards and processes.

It's no coincidence that when we were able to change our processes, we experienced growth. The next five years were night and day compared to the first ten. It started with creating the culture that could attract the right people who believed in the same things. We could then create the processes and support structure required to make it as easy as possible for those employees to serve the customers, but we can never get too comfortable.

This job is never complete. Just because things are running smoothly now, that doesn't mean they can't be improved. The market and technology evolve so fast that if we aren't keeping an eye on how we can improve and continually look for new ways to get ahead, we will most likely be left behind. We never lose sight of that and work to improve our processes, but that requires change and learning how to energize the entire Alpha team to improve the way we do things.

ENCOURAGING CONTINUOUS IMPROVEMENT

There's a difference between letting people do things their own way and being flexible to allow them to improve upon the process. When you start any business, you come in with a unique perspective and set of ideas. You have a clear vision and are responsible for implementing that vision, but that doesn't mean there isn't a better way to do things. That's why soliciting feedback from team members is so important.

We know we don't have all the answers, so by being flexible we allow our people to do things more efficiently and come up with inventive ideas to improve our processes, so we can continue growing.

One of those employees who stepped up was Jason Vogelbaugh, our director of business development. He was responsible for breaking down large projects and developing a proposal for three different companies, but there was a disconnect between the parties involved. It created inefficiencies that made it impossible to respond and turn-around change requests in a short period. The situation finally came to a head when Jason tried coordinating the proposals for a large university project. The existing process for creating a proposal and responding to bid requests was very labor intensive and subject to errors, which made it risky for the business. Jason leveraged the esti-mating system and processes to create a new approach. Over time that became Alpha's takeoff to proposal (T2P) process.

When working within the traditional industry framework, the salespeople had grown used to creating their own proposals. Because there wasn't any consistency at the beginning of the process, it was difficult for our engineers and people working in the field to execute with any consistency. There was typically one meeting where the sales-people conveyed that vision to the engineers, who often never spoke to each other again. The takeoff process was being done twice, and, as expected, there was often miscommunication.

The problem was that when you bid for projects, you must live with the plans, specifications, and quote. It becomes a bible, and the engineers execute the project as they envision it, but we can't just throw a bunch of money out there when competing for the work. And once we win the project, the engineers might submit new drawings or be forced to change things up from the previous proposal at the last minute—sometimes starting over entirely. This was almost impossible to keep tabs on manually while trying to communicate those changes to the execution team so they could integrate them into the design phase. Jason was left to sift through so much paperwork that there was no good way to ensure he caught all those changes.

Meanwhile the engineers were executing a vision that was quite different from what the salespeople pictured and relayed to the customer. When the finished product was much different than what the customer was expecting, the salespeople and engineers were left pointing the finger at each other. Neither took responsibility, and the customer wasn't going to pay for the changes that needed to be made, so the burden fell on our shoulders.

The solution was to create a process that was integrated from beginning to end, but before we could leverage technology, we had to shift the company's culture and change the way things had been done for decades. We all started looking for potential technology solutions in the marketplace, and on the same day, we independently arrived at the same software solution used in the construction industry to mark up and track changes.

With Jason, Phil, Mike, and Jeff Miller working with the two of us, we came up with a way to automate the process of creating an estimate and drafting a proposal. It broke it down into steps, and, more importantly, it streamlined everything to make it consistent. That process is now called the "takeoff to proposal," or T2P, and it's how our engineers work today.

If engineers will be the ones to execute the proposal, why not allow them to figure out what it will look like and develop it, so the salesperson can present to the client precisely what we are going to build? So instead of your spouse explaining their vision for the deck and leaving you to execute it on your own, they go with you to purchase the material and draw up the plans. That way, each of you has a better idea of exactly how it will look, and you are on the same page from day one.

That was the beginning, and the process continued to evolve out of the need to react to different scopes of work in a short timeframe. Today there is consistency in how we create the proposal and execute it, and from the customer perspective, there is a consistent deliverable. When changes need to be made, a new process called the "phase of completed drawings" helps us identify and track those changes.

Another big piece fell into place when Schneider bolstered its software tools leveraging internet and network connections to give our field engineers the ability to access these programs remotely, so by the time they got to the site, everything was already set up. It also meant that team members living in different areas could work on projects without traveling to that area and be just as effective as if they were there. That further cut down on man hours. The more we invest from a programming and analytics standpoint, the more efficient we can make our employees and the more effectively they can serve our customers.

These systems reduce our risk while maximizing our profit. They also make our services more valuable to the customer. People in our industry had been trying to do something about these problems for years and said that it couldn't be done, but we found a way to get it done. Now it's something that sets us apart.

Leaders like Jason, Zach, Dan, Phil, Mike, and Jeff have stepped up in ways that allowed us to utilize technology to aid our growth so we could move forward. This is just another example of why it's so important we get feedback from our team because we heavily rely on that feedback to drive change. We can't just expect to do that from the top; it needs to be built into the organization. We want our employees to bring us ideas and add value by questioning and opera-tionally improving how we execute and provide services and solutions.

CREATING EFFICIENT SYSTEMS, PROCESSES, AND STANDARDS

It goes back to our vision of eliminating barriers. If an employee sees something that can be improved or that is holding them back from being more efficient or getting to the next level, we want them to bring that to our attention. Nobody gets penalized or criticized for that. If those ideas are constructive and can improve the process, we welcome that input with open arms. We actually thrive on it and rely on it to drive the business. It's connected to our philosophy of never being satisfied and striving for continuous improvement. That helps us grow and bring quality solutions to our customers. We've implemented some great ideas from our employees, such as bolstering our customer project support teams. If an idea doesn't work, it doesn't work, but we must be open to trying new things because our business involves constant change and constant improvement, so we can provide better solutions for our customers.

SETTING A STANDARD
By Mike Boogemans: Director of Technical Solutions

If you want to program an area unit to control the temperature coming out at fifty-five degrees all the time, it's amazing how many different ways you can do that, but we don't want our people doing it differently. We want them doing it one way. Standardization is my passion and my wheelhouse.

I started at Alpha in 2006 after moving to Illinois from Vancouver to be with my future wife. I had worked in controls for seventeen years but liked how I could start as a service engineer and didn't have anyone reporting to me. Six years after that, I stepped up when one of Alpha's senior engineers left the company, and I took over one of its biggest jobs in Rockford. That's when I showed what I was capable of and started to move up.

Over the past thirty years, I've fallen on my face enough to get a pretty good idea of what works and what doesn't. When Alpha started standardizing its processes, some of the veterans who might have been stuck in their ways had already retired, so most of the people I worked with were those I had taught, and they often didn't know any other way to do things.

Once a standard is set, that doesn't mean it can't be modified or updated. I looked back at the standards we set six years ago, and we've probably revised most of them twelve times. I'm constantly trying to figure out how we can improve our process to become more efficient. If I'm doing something that takes five minutes, how can I get that down to four or three minutes? It may not seem like much, but it adds up and makes the team faster, more efficient, and more accurate, while cutting down the cost for the customer. This is especially true as everyone wants to become more energy efficient. We never used to think about that, but today we're constantly trying to save our customers money. That requires thinking outside the box while still making the building comfortable.

We do that by constantly tweaking our standards, but that doesn't mean we wait for something to go wrong. It also doesn't mean that my way is the only way or the best way to do things. Nobody likes a dictatorship, so I must be open-minded. I never want to preach, so I'll often ask my guys, "Hey, how should we do this?"

They'll come to me with ideas. They might only have ten years of experience, but I still bounce ideas off them and listen to their suggestions. Sometimes I'll put the whole team together and ask them to make me a list of all the things they wish they did or didn't do or could have done better, so we can make sure to incorporate all those changes. It's not just my wish list; it's everyone's.

A standard is only good if everyone knows to follow it, and that's why Microsoft OneDrive has been so effective at keeping everyone updated. All our standards are in OneDrive, where our employees have access. That way, if I make a change, it shows up on there immediately. We tell our people that when starting a new project, don't automatically do something the way you might have done it six months ago. Check the standards and build from there because that's our latest and greatest.

We used to hold monthly sessions called Alpha Knowledge and Reinforcement Sessions—AKRS. They were on the first Friday of every month, and we got everyone together on Microsoft Teams to go through all these changes and make sure everyone understood. We even recorded those sessions and saved them on OneDrive, so people could go back and watch those videos. Those videos were later used as training sessions to help bring new people up to speed, but eventually even those would be outdated.

I like to say that our standards mature. I make it a point to test the crap out of any new standard on the test board and live panel, but the odd mistake gets through. We don't always get it right the first time. Once we hear about a problem, if it's minor, we make a note and let people know. If it's more serious, we stop right there to fix the standard and send out an email to the team with the new version, so they can fix or update the work they've already done. It takes time to iron out all the bugs and hiccups. That can get some people upset, but I have to remind them to be patient. This is a process, and it takes time for it to mature.

ALLOWING ROOM FOR ORGANIC CHANGE

Change comes in different forms. That includes eliminating barriers, creating opportunities, and leveraging technology. It might involve hiring an outside consultant or investing in intellectual property. Over a decade ago, we were introduced to a valuable technological solution by our peer group, InsideIQ. That group has been around for thirty-five years, started what's called the Independent Representatives Council in the Barber-Colman days, and today has members from all over the globe. We've created great friendships within this group, but it's also a great resource that allows technical experts, salespeople, and business leaders to share best practices. When some folks out in Massachusetts brought an idea to our attention that could solve an issue we were having, we immediately implemented it to improve our efficiency. We know that we can't do it alone, so if we learn of a process or system that can help us grow, we'll do our due diligence and see if we can implement it. We're fast-paced, agile, and willing to try something new because if it works, we can leverage that for our other customers. To truly make lasting change and improve for the better, we know that we must learn something new, but it can't happen all at once.

Someone once said that change in business is like trying to change the tires on a bus while the bus is still moving. Not only is it not easy to do, but since you don't have the luxury of a pit stop, you can't change all the tires at the same time. It's a long game. When you run a marathon, there are checkpoints before the finish line. You can't put your head down and expect to muscle your way to the end. You must pace yourself and plan. It's the exact same way in business. We must look at all four quarters and examine the actions that need to be taken along the way to get where we want to go. We're in agreement about that type of thinking, which has become part of our DNA, but we've also learned to accept that it's not always going to be pretty.

Not every idea will work or be the right fit for us. Sometimes there is a period of adjustment, or we might have to get worse before we get better. We've made miscalculations along the way and put the wrong people in the wrong roles. Luckily none of those miscues was catastrophic or damaged the company. They were more setbacks and missed opportunities that negatively impacted our profit, but dwelling on those miscues doesn't do anyone any good. The moment is gone, and there is nothing you can do about it. The best advice we've ever gotten was to take five minutes to be upset, but then reflect on what happened and see what we can learn from it. We know we'll get another chance, so if we want to improve and come out on top next time, it's essential to understand how. We must be quick to adjust and modify.

The opposite is also true, and we need to take the same approach when things work out in our favor. We take only five minutes to congratulate ourselves and assess why we won. That's important because it will be difficult to replicate that success if we don't know why we won.

It's human nature to extend that reflection period when things are going well and we win—maybe even take a little more time to revel in the victory—but we can't afford to rest on our laurels. As soon as things are working well, we take a step back, find the weakest point in our process, and start working on that. It's like shaking a tree to see what falls out. The two of us have consistently taken that approach and always ask ourselves, "What

> *As soon as things are working well, we take a step back, find the weakest point in our process, and start working on that.*

can we improve next? What's the next thing going to be?" We can't ever lose sight of what's up ahead on the horizon.

The goal is to make continuous incremental improvement. That's how the organization grows and becomes stronger. We can't control everything, but we're doing everything a business can do and taking advantage of all the tools at our disposal. That's what differentiates us from our competitors.

Big companies look at changes like these, and all they see is that it's going to take four or five years, so they are more reluctant to change direction, but we've never been afraid to look at what we could do differently. If you don't start now, you'll never get there. We acknowledge that it will take some time and a lot of work but also recognize that the right change will be worthwhile for the organization in the long run. That's what we choose to focus on, which gives us the conviction to see it through.

These systems and processes we've put in place have helped us grow the business more than threefold, and for an established company in an established market and territory, we feel very proud of this accomplishment. They completely changed the way we did business because we wouldn't have otherwise been able to do more work as quickly or accurately. We've set up the company today to bring people in with different perspectives and skillsets and teach them the functions, so they can build on what we're trying to do. We wouldn't be where we are today without key people living our mission statement and having everyone working as a team to buy into our purpose and what we're trying to do. It's fun to sit back and watch what some of our young engineers are doing. They're building relationships with customers from the beginning and fulfilling the dream we had long ago.

We haven't reached our critical mass, but we're getting close. And we know we're doing something right when we have inspired our multibillion-dollar partner to follow suit with some of our processes. With everyone working together and on the same page, we can focus on delivering quality products and services to our customers. They've come to expect a certain quality from Alpha, and we've set out not only to meet those expectations, but also to exceed them.

CHAPTER 5
SETTING AND EXCEEDING
EXPECTATIONS

I n 2011 Jason bumped into a friend at a trade show who was on the board of a retirement community in Bloomington, Illinois. The board happened to be looking to replace its cooling tower, and the friend asked if Jason had any suggestions. It would be the third time the community replaced the tower since 1978, so each one was lasting less than twenty years.

When Jason went out there, he saw their system was already set up for a geothermal well field. Making the switch from a tower to a well field was a radical idea that required a significant investment, but it did provide many advantages. It was more stable, so they wouldn't have to worry about replacing the system again for fifty years. It was also more environmentally friendly, and with the cooling tower gone, it freed up room on the loading dock. Most importantly, it would improve the quality of life for the residents. And since this was a facility for the elderly, maintaining a stable environment was essential. They agreed.

Up to that point, Alpha had never done a million-dollar negotiated project, and this was a $7 million project, so it was a monumental step forward for the company. To mitigate the risk, we partnered up for the well field, mechanical work, and electrical work, so we could focus only on the controls piece and the overall project coordination.

That job was only the beginning. A few months later, we finally convinced the American Federation of Labor and Congress of Industrial Organizations (AFL-CIO) in Springfield, Illinois, to modernize its facility, but instead of the $50,000 upgrade we had been proposing, we got the organization to see the benefit of a $250,000, more energy-efficient upgrade that would save more money in the long run. It even committed to the work being done during an election year when the AFL-CIO was its busiest.

The most significant boon in our energy solutions business occurred in 2014 after meeting with the superintendent of a Bloomington, Illinois, school district. There were nine separate buildings that required modernization, but before he agreed to make a significant investment, he wanted us to prove that we could deliver what we proposed by working first on one of the smaller elementary school buildings. We drew up a $290,000 proposal for a sixty-thousand-square-foot building whose energy bill at the time was $103,000 a year. With our solution we could save them over $40,000 a year and help them earn back $130,000 in utility incentives.

Over the following year, we closely monitored the job and went back to make tweaks when necessary to ensure we hit our target. When the superintendent saw we could deliver the savings we promised, we went to work on three more of their buildings in 2015, another three in 2016, and the final two in 2017. Not only did that project at Bloomington High School earn it the largest single incentive Nicor Gas ever paid out—$425,000—but it also went on to win the Illinois Governor's Sustainability Award in 2017.

That attracted the attention of Unit 5, the much bigger neighboring school district. When we presented what we could offer, the district leadership was hooked and asked us to take a look at one of its junior high buildings, which was in a lot of trouble. The systems were forty years old and had never been upgraded, so they were literally falling apart. A six-inch water main had recently burst and flooded the school. The administrators were already considering a geothermal retrofit with another company and asked our opinion about an alternative solution. After we analyzed the building, we gave them our honest opinion: the geothermal retrofit was the way to go. The board was shocked because we weren't advocating for our project—we advocated for the right thing to do.

We didn't win that project, but our assessment and recommendation gained us so much credibility with the administrators that they immediately engaged us in more projects. Since then we've done more than $9 million worth of energy efficiency work for them, and between the incentives and utility savings, they've gotten back almost 50 percent of that.

None of this success was an accident or occurred because of luck. For us to consistently set and exceed expectations, we must have a firm grasp of the scope of work and what it will require of us to complete it. No matter the job, it always begins in the same place—the budget.

THE IMPORTANCE OF CREATING AN ACCURATE BUDGET

The worst thing that ever happened to us in terms of the expectations we put on our business has been Amazon. If you come up with a crazy idea for a home improvement project, you can order everything online and have some materials delivered that same day. No more coming up with a plan and going to multiple stores to search the shelves. You don't even have to leave the house. That attitude has spoiled us, and we've gotten used to getting what we need incredibly quickly, and when we don't, we become impatient. Amazon has set the standard for service that everyone has come to expect, so if we want to have a chance to meet expectations, it starts by creating an accurate budget.

Frank managed the budgeting for the branches and joint ventures back in the corporate days based on the break-even analysis process, which looks at product mix. Most CPA firms that deal with small businesses use a traditional financial framework that only tells you your revenue, cost of goods sold, overhead, and profit. The problem is that you cannot use that information to see if you are on track to reaching your goals. That was why we opted for a break-even analysis format for financial reporting because it better allowed us to track our financial results and see if we were on target, so we could easily adjust. This approach was straightforward and could work with small businesses and large multimillion-dollar businesses. It was so successful back in the corporate days that we did the same thing when we started Alpha.

We have two core businesses—projects and the service business. Service contracts, spot service (unplanned customer work order requests), replacement material for controls, mechanical service, and access controls all fall under the service umbrella. Still, we are very much a project-oriented business as that represents over 80 percent of our revenue. We'd like to get that split down to sixty-forty between projects and services, but both sides of the company are growing significantly. That's a good thing, but it makes it difficult to change the ratio. The revenue cycle is different for each—a new project can last anywhere from two weeks to two years, where we can get a service call in the morning and bill that same afternoon. Profit margins are also different for project and service. We expect higher profit margins for our service business given the higher overhead cost required to support the service business.

Every year we start all over again with a brand-new budget. Before we come up with that number, we must consider the backlog of ongoing projects and new project bookings already in the pipeline that will be completed during that year. That gives us a starting point. We then devise a plan for what new projects we'll book that year. Jason, who runs our business development team, puts together a pipeline report of which customers we're targeting, what the probability is we're going to close them, and when. Every month projects come in, and projects go out, so we must stay on top of it all.

What makes projects more difficult to budget than service is that we must add people gradually and make those people productive. We've ditched the corporate mentality about limiting headcounts, because that creates restraints. We go in the opposite direction and hire more people in advance, so we're overstaffed to a certain extent. That helps us meet project schedules on time and achieve growth. It's about resource allocation, so we also do individual department budgets, which helps us figure out how many people we'll need to serve each project and how many billable hours it will require. Since we're labor intensive and not capital intensive, labor is a big chunk of what we do. That's our capital, so we must know our labor cost going in. At the beginning of the year, we incorporate all these pieces to develop a targeted, high-level prediction for what we will convert into revenue for the year.

> We've ditched the corporate mentality about limiting headcounts, because that creates restraints.

We come very close to meeting that number, but there are always surprises because nobody has any way of knowing what might happen in a given year. The economy, the geopolitical environment, supply chain issues, and any number of outside factors can throw our budget out of whack and impact our margins. That's why we use a series of key performance indicators (KPIs) to track our progress to monitor where we are every month compared to the target budget we set. We set the plan and monitor it to stay on track, and if we see any red flags, we can adjust and see what we could do differently. We either back off or push ahead, depending on how much work we actually do. And if we aren't meeting those numbers, we can see if it's volume based, if it's trouble with cost, execution, or overspending on overhead. We home in on that and drill down into each of those pieces. It's gotten so precise that we now have a two-quarter warning of any upcoming issues. That gives us time to refocus our efforts. We can also effectively communicate that information with our banking and bonding company to help us maintain those key business relationships. Without those systems and processes in place, that would require more resources and time.

Alpha Project Backlog Overhead Coverage
Target 60%

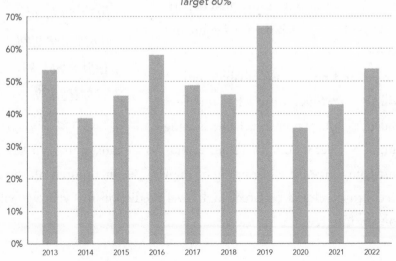

GETTING THE ENTIRE TEAM ON BOARD

The two of us oversaw this process on our own until 2019 when we started sharing the financials with our directors and leadership team. They monitor our progress and help us stay focused on the plan. They need to know these KPIs, manage the people below them, and track their billable hours because there is no middle management. It's an entire team effort with each person working within their own discipline while focusing on the bigger picture. Everyone contributes to the different phases of the project. Since quality growth is a big chunk of compensation for the leadership team, they can't be in the dark about the budget and what we're trying to accomplish as a company.

It comes down to communication, so everyone understands the financial pieces at play and the key drivers of our business. It means we now schedule virtual and onsite meetings for the central Illinois, northern Illinois, and Wisconsin teams to provide year-to-date updates on the status of financial and work plans. Another benefit of the onsite meetings is the networking and team building that help solidify relationships through face-to-face discussions. These meetings also give us an opportunity to talk about future plans.

We've even created bonuses for our key people based on our profit. That makes our internal expectations—specifically the budget we set—more important than ever. Our directors and leadership team know their targets and drive that down through the organization. They are constantly looking to improve resource allocation and ensure they stay on top of the billable hours they are responsible for. This has helped them update our time reporting system, making the operation more efficient.

These bonus plans have worked out great so far because we've been growing, but if not managed properly, these could be demotivating, so we must continue to set an accurate and fair budget. Sometimes we've made short-term decisions to take less of a return because we know we can expect a long-term benefit. If we're going to make investments in growth, that might mean our profit before taxes will be lower, so we always have to measure the pros and cons. And we always ask ourselves if we're being fair to our employees and the company because it all goes back to fairness. That's why we make everyone aware of the plan, so they know what they need to do. When the plan changes, we have a conversation to let everyone know why and what's going on. When we become crystal clear on our expectations for the company, we can more effectively convey realistic expectations to our customers.

WHAT THE CUSTOMER CAN EXPECT FROM ALPHA

In the age of Amazon, we're lucky that our customers don't have unrealistic expectations. Only one time were we in a situation where we had a disagreement with a client about paying for completed work that we couldn't resolve. We cut ties with that client, but that rarely happens, and whenever we sense a potential issue on the horizon, we get out in front of it as soon as possible. We were once told that not every customer is meant to be *our* customer. This was a classic example of that sage advice. It starts in the very beginning by setting and maintaining a strict schedule. That's often the difference between setting the expectations and having expectations set for us.

Scheduling our new projects can be tricky because we aren't always the ones who establish the timeline, especially when bidding on a project. Timelines are often set by the general contractor and the facility owner we're working with. That schedule can vary based on the size and specifications of the project, but it's all precise. We look closely at what we must do to meet the customer needs and deliver value, and then we work backward to determine the date while also considering the existing commitments we have to our other customers. So before we even start a project, we've laid the groundwork and know the scope of the work. It's not just timelines we need to consider when setting expectations for the customer; we also need to budget, so we know exactly what each project will cost and how many man hours are required.

Once that contract is signed, we immediately begin executing because we must meet those terms on that date, or there will be financial penalties for every day we don't complete work. We're committed, so we must deliver, but in the early days of Alpha, we often found ourselves behind the eight ball.

In the early days, when we received the contract, the design would have to be approved before we could order material and begin programming. This left us minimal margin for error, and making these deadlines was killing us, especially when working at a school or a location where the work needed to be completed by a precise date. We would benefit from more time, but since we couldn't extend the deadline, we took back control by looking internally and changing our execution model. That's when we implemented standard programs, so we didn't have to start each project from scratch. We could apply a specific design and programming to different projects, which immediately sped up the process. We rearranged the way we did things. We looked through every nook and cranny of the process, and by assigning our

> Though we do everything possible to avoid delays, the real skill is learning how to make up that time elsewhere.

resources more effectively and leveraging technology, we could find that extra time needed to make those deadlines, but even then, rarely did anything ever go according to plan.

Delays are inevitable, and even though we do everything possible to avoid delays, the real skill is learning how to make up that time elsewhere. We might get a week or two-week extension, but the completion date won't move in most cases. Whenever a problem arises or there is a change in the plan, we document and communicate that change, so we can stay out in front of any issues because the slightest problem could snowball if left unchecked, and that can impact our budget and delay the job.

One of the rare exceptions is if the delay is owner related. For example, if the owner needs to do asbestos removal in an area of the facility, that might cause a delay. There are workarounds, and we divert resources to other parts of the project, but something like that is out of our control. We faced this situation recently when upgrading our systems in a hospital because we could only work in certain areas at specific times and not contaminate the area we were in. That required extensive coordination with the customer and subcontractors to get the job done. There is always a solution. We must ensure we are nimble enough to adapt when necessary. In twenty years we've only missed one deadline, so that doesn't happen often.

DEALING WITH EXTERNAL CIRCUMSTANCES

Looking for ways to avoid potential issues is built into our mindset and culture. It goes back to our vision statement about eliminating barriers. We've become proactive and dedicated to getting the job done right the first time. It's true for the expectations we set for our new projects and service business. We've already hammered home that we're not done with a service job until the paperwork has been filed and the project is out of warranty. That means the infrastructure system is up and running and is capable of doing so for all four seasons. We operate in the Midwest and live in a climate where it's hot for part of the year, cold for the other, and often fluctuates between the two without warning.

Our service business faces a different set of challenges, and one way we attempt to stay out in front of those challenges is with our policy of zero callbacks. That means we do it right the first time. Our people take pride in the solutions and services they deliver. They don't want to let the customer down because they've made a commitment, and that's baked into our culture. It's also not in anyone's interest to go back and fix something that was not done right the first time, especially our employees. They've already put the tools away and filed the paperwork. It's out of sight and out of mind, so getting back into the headspace needed to resolve an issue is challenging.

This zero-callbacks policy is something else we can't take credit for because it actually preceded Alpha and was part of the expectations Frank had tried to instill across the corporate branches. We just brought it with us when we went off on our own. Sure, there is the odd exception, and we never reach absolute zero callbacks, but it's about setting expectations and following through to hold people accountable. When we say zero callbacks, what we really mean is best in class. And just because we come close to achieving zero callbacks, that doesn't mean we don't have a system in place to touch base and follow up to ensure there aren't any lingering issues. We want our people to remain committed to our customers and grinding out the day. In that area our people consistently exceed our expectations.

Managing expectations comes down to communication internally with our employees and externally with our subcontractors and the customers. We're all in this together. Nobody is happy about delays and problems, but the sooner we all know when something goes wrong, the quicker and more efficiently we can work together to find a solution.

We may not be in control of all the external circumstances, but through preparation (and our systems and processes), we ensure that we not only set the expectations, but also deliver and exceed those expectations by providing better quality customer solutions. Much of that has to do with the products and technology supplied by Schneider, but we're responsible for creating the projects, implementing them, and providing the end solution to the customer. That's a unique process that we continually strive to improve upon.

HOW TO DELIVER LASTING RESULTS

As industry standards change, we incorporate that into our technology, validate its effectiveness, and implement it. If we're going to be that trusted advisor to our customers, we need to stay ahead of the curve to bring them practical solutions today, while still positioning them for the future. We're always trying to make our projects more energy efficient because that means we save our customers money on their utilities.

We joke that we sell smart thermostats. There is some truth to that on a very basic level, but what we really do is help our customers maximize the efficiency of their buildings and optimize the comfort of their occupants. When people are comfortable, they are more productive. The right energy solutions and technology have even been shown to increase the value of a building. Technology is changing faster than ever, so the equipment is constantly being upgraded. We must stay on top of that for our customers, but that doesn't mean every upgrade and solution is a good fit for every customer.

If you buy a television, you own it for a while, even when newer models with better technology emerge. It's not practical to buy a new television every time a new one comes out with more streaming functions, but eventually you decide to move on. The products and services we sell at Alpha work in a similar way. Our products are part of the infrastructure of a building, and the digital devices and control systems we install will last twenty years or longer. The primary function of many of these systems doesn't change much. The types of systems and sizes of the facilities differ, and there are different versions with different technologies, but the functionality of these systems remains the same. There are systems we installed back in the 1980s that are still up and running. Like a good pair of shoes, they may not be in style anymore, but they fit great and they're comfortable, so you don't want to get rid of them. The good news is that these systems last a long time. The bad news is that they last a long time.

Before we had digital controls, everything broke down more often. Today our equipment and systems could have five-year warranties. Once we get the system installed and commissioned, it's very reliable, but we still need a facility optimization agreement because it's a software-based system that requires cybersecurity and firmware updates. These agreements are very important. We need to provide the customer information and constantly monitor the system as you would a car when you get it serviced at the dealership. Those mechanics can identify immediately what's wrong. That's what we're trying to replicate with our technology.

This becomes especially important since our customers no longer have those veterans in their organization who understand these systems. The people in these roles aren't always familiar with the equipment, so we need to help them run their facilities and, more importantly, not waste energy while keeping everyone comfortable in the building. That involves training their employees on how to regulate temperature, humidity, and a host of other factors. These systems are complex, so even though they are reliable and can last twenty years, they do require software and firmware upgrades and maintenance. There are incredible modern features and functions today, such as viewing and accessing the controls through a mobile device.

If we install the system but do not have a facility optimization agreement in place to maintain it, the benefit to the customer will decline over time. They simply won't get the same return on investment and will have much higher operating costs than if we are able to properly maintain them and provide proactive support.

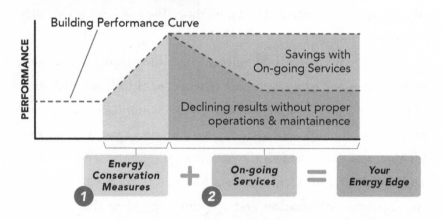

A service contract means that we get renewable work, but, more importantly, we get to maintain that long-term relationship with the customer. We want to be there to negotiate that contract for additional work or an upgrade down the road, not have it go out to bid to one of our competitors. Technology changes rapidly, and some form of modernization is required every seven or eight years. When investing in technologies, our technology partner has considered the customers' perspective and desire to maximize their return over time, but these systems still need to be modernized. Updates, new features, and technological enhancements improve the connection between the system and the outside world to make them more user friendly. This cuts down on any unexpected problems.

We make sure to use that term, "modernize," instead of using words like "update" and "obsolete." If someone says you need to update your TV because it's obsolete, you're going to say, "Nothing's wrong with my TV. It does everything I need. I don't need to update anything." But if someone comes to you and says, "You should modernize your TV," it gets you thinking in a completely different way. And people like Phil, Mike, and their teams have helped us modernize our customer experience.

These digital systems are much more reliable and durable than they were twenty years ago, but that doesn't mean they don't need to be properly maintained. However, when the equipment runs correctly and there aren't any problems, nobody notices it, and customers assume they don't need that service agreement. One customer modernized its systems, but we could never get that customer to take the next step and follow up with preventative maintenance. That ends up having a massive cost in the long run because the equipment can only work how it's supposed to for so long without being properly maintained. That's the catch, but those customers are more the exception than the rule. While listening to customers' needs, we're tailoring that offering to them. So if their people don't yet have a firm grasp on the technology and the equipment, that might mean that our people are on site more often.

In 2020 we were given the opportunity to bring our energy solutions business to the next level by partnering with Ideal Impact in Grapevine, Texas. Ideal Impact has helped us add value to many of our largest energy solutions customers by saving them more on their utilities than they had with other programs. Its founder, Wes McDaniel, is the Michael Jordan of energy solutions, so it feels like the best in the industry is teaching us how to do what we do, but better. It took our leaders about fifteen seconds to see value in what Ideal Impact offered and get on board. It's been transformational for our business so far, and we're only scratching the surface.

Not only does this partnership help us execute, but Ideal Impact also helps us better understand how to get this message out to our customers. We want to utilize Ideal Impact as much as possible to maximize potential energy savings because every dollar the customer doesn't have to spend on a utility is a dollar that customer can use to improve its business and further its mission, be it teaching, governing, or producing something.

There is always something to learn and improve upon. The most significant change in the past five years has been the impact of cyber theft, hacking, and ransoming of data. Since our equipment is part of a building's infrastructure, we must now protect against the outside world being able to penetrate that infrastructure. One recent example is the hacking of Target. Myriad bad decisions made by contractors with inadequate security led to this, but Target was vulnerable because its financial system was not isolated from its control system. The systems weren't on local area networks (LAN) and didn't utilize virtual private networks (VPN). So once the hackers got into Target's network, they were on the same highway and had access to the servers that hosted the company's financial and customer information.

> The most significant change in the past five years has been the impact of cyber theft, hacking, and ransoming of data.

We've received inquiries from our customers about these cybersecurity issues, so we need to let them know what we're doing on our end. We've started investing more in cybersecurity and have done a complete audit of our own business. It begins with us, so we've taken action to watch for cyber threats within our own company. We've changed our internal practices that everyone in the company needs to comply with. We're doing the same for the solutions we provide our customers and updating their systems with more advanced cybersecurity. We always want to stay one step ahead regarding the modernization process and any new IT, so we continue doing more than the average company. And since we are in a smaller market, it allows us to apply these technologies differently, giving us a bit of an edge.

Our goal always remains the same: provide customers with the most energy-efficient equipment and solutions to save money and keep them happy. If customers aren't satisfied, we won't retain them. Customers work with Alpha because they know we're going to get the job done on time and on budget without any unexpected costs. The equipment provided by Schneider Electric does much of the heavy lifting, but it's not nearly as effective if we don't have the right people to install, maintain, and monitor that equipment. Our competitors can have the same technology, but they don't have our people. As long as we have the right people in the right roles, give them the necessary tools, and hold them accountable to comply with the systems and processes in place, that's the best thing we can do to ensure we continue to meet expectations—for the customer and for Alpha. That doesn't mean that issues won't arise because there is always something that can go wrong. Seasons change, and supply-chain issues can throw a wrench in the works, but it becomes much easier to overcome those challenges when everyone is on the same page.

CHAPTER 6

STANDING YOUR GROUND WHEN FACED WITH ADVERSITY

In 2005, two years after being in business, we finally landed our first big million-dollar project when we won the bid for the Winnebago County criminal justice center in Rockford, Illinois. We were still growing, so this was a big risk that could make or break the business, but we knew that keeping that customer would lead to more work because the county was looking to upgrade the systems in the five other buildings on its campus. This was our chance to take the business to the next level, but we soon found ourselves in a situation that could set us back years.

When overseeing the branches at Invensys, the leadership didn't do a consistent job of investing in project-management resources for large projects. Their project managers wouldn't attend early project meetings. They never engaged early enough on site to understand the general conditions and overall project scopes for other contractors. They didn't build relationships with the architects, general contractors, and electrical and mechanical contractors. So once we landed the justice center, the two of us made sure that we were involved from the very beginning. We also looped in Jason, our operations manager,

MORE THAN A MISSION STATEMENT

and Sarah, our design engineer. Everything went smoothly until about four months into the project. During a design review meeting, Sarah pointed out how there was no smoke control in the specifications.

Any facility that houses permanent occupants is required by code to have some form of smoke control. The sprinkler system is the primary defense against fire, but smoke control is a secondary system designed to give people fifteen minutes to escape an area where there is a fire by ventilating that area and providing fresh air. However, you only have fifteen minutes, because when you pump fresh air onto a fire, it burns faster. It's like you're feeding the fire and then pressurizing any floors above and below to contain the smoke, so everyone has time to reach the exits.

The architect and engineer left this spec section out of the bid documents. It was an oversight on their part, but because our team was in those early meetings, we caught this and brought it to everyone's attention. In a meeting with about thirty people, the architects and engineer overseeing the project had to acknowledge that there was a mistake and that this section was left out.

We immediately put in a change order request. When this got back to the ownership of that firm, they realized how much exposure they had, so they tried to pin it on us and say that it was in the bid documents, but because we had been going to the meetings and had established relationships with the engineers, the building's other contractors, and the county, we had everyone's support. We also had all the proper documentation, so we could push back and prove this wasn't our responsibility. Based on the facts, they had no choice but to honor that change order.

It took nine months, and we had to fight for it, but we got the change order approved. That saved the project financially for Alpha. Had we not been in those meetings and caught this oversight early, the situation could have turned nasty. Eventually someone would notice because they wouldn't have gotten approval from the county or the local fire department without the proper smoke control. We may or may not have ended up in the same place, but we would have been in a precarious position. And if we did have to pay for the smoke control addition, it would have set us back several years. That would have been a massive hit for a company our size that had only been in business for two years.

That was our first big project, and it felt like we dodged a bullet. We knew we needed to do things differently after leaving corporate, but that situation hammered the lesson home like nothing else ever could. With every single new job from that moment forward, we made sure to get in early, understand the scope of work, read the documents, and engage with all the other parties to ensure we would deliver what we were responsible for and not have additional work that wasn't included in the original scope forced upon us. Looking back, it was the transition to our T2P process that took the "get to the details early" approach to an important new level.

One of the best ways to handle adversity is to be prepared and do our due diligence to prevent some problems from ever arising. That has become part of our philosophy and has gotten us very far, but, unfortunately, sometimes in our business stuff just happens.

LEARNING HOW TO THINK ON OUR FEET

The Rockford Ice Hogs play in the American Hockey League and are the minor league affiliate of the Chicago Blackhawks. They play their home games at the BMO Harris Bank Center in Rockford. It's a local ten-thousand-seat arena that hosts various concerts and events, but the number-one revenue-generating part of its business is the Ice Hogs because they play thirty-six home games a year between October and April, not counting preseason and playoffs.

The center became our customer in 2013, and a major responsibility was maintaining the skating ice. Arenas host different events, but during hockey season they put the various subfloors over that ice, which remains frozen underneath. So after a hockey game, they put the basketball floor on top of the ice, then remove the floor for the next hockey game. It's much easier to fit the pieces of the basketball court floor together than to freeze and unfreeze the thirteen thousand gallons of water needed to make the ice before every hockey game. But that means you must keep that ice frozen for months at a time. That's done through a chiller system and up to ten miles of pipes zigzagging beneath the arena floor.

The challenge with this arena was that the chiller was over thirty years old. It looked like an old train engine and was probably around from when they first built the building. Replacing it would be the ideal solution, but that would be a significant job that could take months, which meant they wouldn't be able to have access to the ice during that time. That wasn't an option until the hockey season was over. So when we took over service of the arena, we encouraged them to invest $38,000 in necessary maintenance and upkeep, knowing the chiller was at the end of its useful life. We hoped to make it through one more season before we could devise a permanent solution. It looked like we were going to make it, but with a month left, the one thing we all feared would happen happened.

Brent was out of town that weekend, so Zach got the call from our mechanical service supervisor at eleven o'clock at night on Saturday telling him there was a catastrophic failure on the chiller. They had the basketball floor down for the Harlem Globetrotters game the next afternoon, but underneath, the ice was melting, and they had a hockey game on Wednesday. There was nothing we could have done to prevent this. It was just bad luck. The equipment was past its useful life, but none of that mattered. We needed to scramble to come up with a solution to the arena's first and most immediate problem so it could host the basketball game the next day.

Our people told the arena people to pull the floor up because we needed to work throughout the night to find and install a temporary chiller, so we could start making ice again. Our team reached out to contacts throughout the country to secure a temporary chiller. We then worked with the customer's team, local contractors, and a local supply house to provide the labor and materials necessary to install the temporary chiller and have it operational by Monday afternoon. The catch was that we had to park it outside of the facility on a flatbed truck because it wouldn't fit in the mechanical room of the building. Our team also had to get the approval and a special permit from the city of Rockford. Fortunately, while we were focused on the chiller, the arena staff worked through the night removing and reinstalling the basketball flooring, so the Globetrotters could play their game as scheduled on Sunday. Still, there was no guarantee that everything would be ready for the hockey game on Wednesday.

Making ice for an arena is a complex process. First the ice is layered on top of the concrete in thin sheets. Then the lines need to be painted—red lines, blue lines, goal lines, face-off circles, and goal creases. The stencils and decals all need to be carefully painted and laid out before another layer of water is sprayed over the top to freeze it all into place. It's an art, and there is a tiny margin for error. If the ice is too soft, it will get torn up, but if it's too cold, it can crack. There's a lot of science required to get it in that Goldilocks zone. You also need to regulate the arena's temperature to ensure the ice doesn't melt, and that temperature can't change when ten thousand people are inside. This takes a couple of days, so we were in a time crunch.

Hockey was the number-one revenue-generating part of the business for this arena, so it would obviously take a hit if it couldn't host the game. However, what would hurt even more would be the penalties associated with missing a game because of a facility issue. Those fines were astronomical and upwards of six figures. The Ice Hogs were an AHL affiliate, so this was a whole different world, and the conditions couldn't have been more stressful for us.

Brent returned on Monday, and the business manager was still upset when we all sat down for a meeting, but as soon as we brought up work interruption insurance, his demeanor changed. He stopped, took off down the hall, and returned in a completely different mood. "You're a genius! Let me figure this out. This meeting's over. Come back tomorrow." Business interruption insurance meant that costs for the repairs and chiller replacement would be covered by insurance. The next day we started working with their insurance representative. We held up our end, and our guys worked with the customer to control the temperature in the arena to get the job done right. The hockey game on Wednesday went off without a hitch, but we still weren't out of the woods yet.

The temporary ice chiller needed to remain outside for the remainder of the season. That required additional permits and zoning clearances because it was blocking an entire lane of traffic. When the season ended, a few things had to happen over the next couple of months. The permanent chiller needed to be designed to fit the space. The final design included two smaller chillers, which not only provided a better system, but also provided for a backup chiller in case of another failure. That required a series of approvals. Equipment needed to be ordered and installed. We had to redo much of the electrical work to support the new equipment. That meant reconnecting and reprogramming almost everything, but we got it all done over the summer, so the ice was ready to go when the season started again in October. We also had to provide a detailed report of all the technical information to get the insurance claim paid. That went on for months, but a reliable chiller system was installed to ensure we wouldn't have a similar problem for a long time.

That was a horrible situation to be in with a brand-new client. They had just invested in a $38,000 temporary solution that didn't work and experienced a catastrophic failure that could have severely impacted their business. Our entire team came together. We reacted at the moment and worked really hard to solve a big problem in a short amount of time. That didn't go unnoticed, and it's the main reason we still have that client today and continue to have an excellent working relationship.

Not only was that our first big project, but it also jumpstarted our mechanical service business. We had been doing mechanical service and change-out repairs up to that point. We had a small team, so we had never operated as a construction manager or coordinated an entire project, but that's precisely what we did at the arena. We operated as the construction manager and hired a professional engineering firm to collaborate on the chiller design. We hired the subcontractors, and the owner looked to us to deliver the solution on time. We even helped them get a $500,000 check from the insurance company. Doing a project of that magnitude in such a short period set the stage for us to do it again. We were confident we could take on those kinds of projects, so when the opportunity presented itself, we pursued it.

We had tried to get the mechanical service business going before and had invested multiple six figures in getting it off the ground, but it didn't take off the way we had hoped because we didn't have the right people in the right roles. We could never get on the same page with the first two people we hired because they wanted to do things their way and didn't fit into our system. That's when Mike Williams said, "I'd like a shot at this and be the guy in charge." As they say, the third time's the charm because Mike stepped up and knocked it out of the park.

Mike was a team-oriented person who really understood what we were trying to do from a company standpoint. He had been with us for a while, so he was familiar with different facets of our business. He was the perfect man for the job, and our mechanical service business took off from there. We had learned from our past mistakes about what to do and what not to do. Suddenly we were taking on more work and adding more people. That business has grown to $5.2 million today, and even though it remains a small part of what we do, it's a profitable arm of the business that continues to grow, and, most importantly, it allows us to provide more services to our customers. That helps us build those relationships and expand our footprint.

> On the other side of adversity lies opportunity.

On the other side of adversity lies opportunity, and how things unfolded at the BMO Harris Bank Center is the quintessential example of how we solved a problem for our customer and created an opportunity to grow our business in the process. It proved that we could respond in a crisis, but adversity comes in all shapes and sizes, and you never know when it will hit. The best anyone can ever expect to do is be prepared.

HOW DO YOU PREPARE FOR A FUTURE NOBODY CAN PREDICT?

In 2008 we targeted local school districts and landed some big projects. A few years earlier, we had set out to build up our backlog. What neither we nor anybody else could have anticipated was that we would need that backlog. That same year, when the financial crisis hit and other contractors started to struggle, our backlog of projects got us through and helped us continue to grow. So, in 2008, we didn't hunker down and try to survive; we took advantage of the opportunity to get ahead of our competition.

Outsiders might call it luck, but we know it all goes back to our growth philosophy. From the beginning we've always asked ourselves, "What will we do next?" That mindset allowed us to grow the company and become more efficient at leveraging technology. By 2008 we had transitioned the business away from the traditional plan and spec work and tiptoed into more energy-justified selling. These were projects where we could engage in a dialogue and negotiate with customers. We would talk to them about how they could improve their infrastructure. This expanded the scope of our business. Add our backlog of projects to the mix, and we were growing at a time when most everyone else was struggling. It wasn't luck as much as it was preparation.

Nobody saw the 2008 financial crisis coming, just like nobody could have predicted the COVID-19 pandemic twelve years later in 2020. Once again we were prepared simply because we had adhered to our growth philosophy. However, that doesn't mean we didn't have to sweat it out and learn to adapt like everyone else.

Nobody knew what was happening when the world locked down in March 2020. Just like in 2008, we had a solid backlog, but that didn't do us any good when we couldn't work. All service stopped instantaneously, and we saw a 25 percent reduction in that business. Many customers told us, "Don't send your people into my building. We'll call you if anything breaks."

We were worried that our job sites would shut down and had no idea if we'd be able to collect on our receivables because we still had to pay for materials and subcontractors. Since we couldn't work, we didn't know what to do with our people. The scope of our business had suddenly changed, but we didn't panic. We stayed the course and did what we always do: look for the opportunity amid the adversity.

We were eventually declared an essential business, which meant we could continue to operate remotely but also work on customer and job sites following defined COVID protocols. For us to move to a hybrid remote work business model, we needed to make two things happen. First we had to get laptops into the hands of our business operations people, so they could access these systems remotely. That was easy. Second we had to figure out how many concurrent soft VPN licenses we owned. We owned fifty, and it turned out we needed one hundred. Altogether that took two hours, and that was how long some of our people were down, so we didn't miss a beat. That's what COVID cost us: two hours.

We had already installed digital control systems with remote visualization. That meant we already had access to our customers' systems. Our people could still support and serve our customers, even if they weren't on site or speaking to them personally. The customer could call with a problem, and our people could troubleshoot remotely. If our people had to visit the site, which did happen, they could schedule a time that worked and was safest for everyone. Communication was crucial, and every one of our team members had to be on the same page with each other, the customers, and our contractors to ensure we were in compliance.

Everything went smoothly because we continually invest in technology, standards, processes, and our people. A few months earlier, we had put in place an effective time-tracking system for every one of our field people, so they knew exactly how much time they were spending on various projects, which allowed us to work more efficiently. We didn't know anything about COVID and didn't put any of this in place because we knew what was coming. It was all done at the end of the previous year so the team leaders could ensure their people were spending their time responsibly. It was just one of the many decisions we made over the last twenty years to leverage technology, grow the business, and put our people in a position to work more effectively and efficiently. That helped them thrive when circumstances suddenly changed. The fact that it allowed us to remain fully functional during an unpredictable disaster such as COVID was simply an ancillary benefit and the result of our forward thinking. But nobody had any idea how things would turn out in the future, so we couldn't get comfortable.

Every Monday during the pandemic, we met with the entire team to tell them what we knew and were doing as a company. Meanwhile we spent hours every week communicating with our peers to learn more about what was happening worldwide. Once a week Schneider Electric hosted what we started calling "cocktail hour." It quickly turned into cocktail three hours where we met on Teams with our partners from all over the country to discuss what was happening in our business. We talked about problems, solutions, and potential opportunities. We always made it a point to attend those Teams calls, because if we

> *Every Monday during the pandemic, we met with the entire team to tell them what we knew and were doing as a company.*

125

could take only one piece of information and use that to improve our business, it would be a win. COVID was a unique situation where all of us were in the same boat, no matter where we were in the world. That information sharing and feedback from people with all different perspectives were invaluable and helped us stay on top of everything as new data emerged. We just made sure we were nimble enough to pivot at a moment's notice if need be.

As the pandemic dragged on, we started slowly moving our essential business operations people back into our facilities where they could work more efficiently. We didn't need everyone back in the building, so many of our employees continued to work remotely. The two of us continued to work from home, which didn't change how we did things, but something very interesting started to happen. Suddenly the value our customers placed on our services began to change. They needed us, and we were getting more and more calls about ensuring their buildings were safe and properly ventilated.

If you make cars and tell people that fuel efficiency matters, they might not pay that much attention when gas is two dollars a gallon. But when gas skyrockets to six dollars a gallon, they realize how it matters. It works the same exact way with the air quality of a building. We had been talking about the importance of this for years, and it's why we invested so much in technology, but for a long time, it fell on deaf ears until we were in a crisis. Now everyone was concerned about the air quality and proper ventilation in their buildings.

While our competitors were trying to figure out how they would survive tomorrow, we knew that we had today and tomorrow covered because of our preparation and philosophy. What we didn't have covered was a year, two years, or five years down the road. That's when we did something counterintuitive by making a quarter-of-a-million-dollar investment with Ideal Impact, so we could play ball with the

Michael Jordan of our business. Many people thought we were nuts and didn't buy into what we were doing, but luckily they didn't have to because it wasn't their money.

This was an opportunity to take the business to the next level. Was it a risk? Yes, but just as in '08, we had a substantial backlog, and that 25 percent drop we saw in the service business rebounded quickly as people started to figure out how they could operate with the various protocols. We could afford to take that risk when our competition wasn't in the position to do the same. The competition might have been weak then, but we had the wherewithal, mindset, and commitment to take that risk because we believed it was the right thing to do.

As the world emerged from COVID, we were suddenly faced with a new potential crisis in 2022—supply-chain issues. That impacted when the equipment arrived at job sites and if we could complete jobs by the deadline. Everyone had these problems, and clients were aware there could be potential delays, but we knew from experience that we could consistently execute more effectively when prepared. In this case being prepared meant how we set the budget. The problem was that changing the budget could impact bonuses for our people, so we first needed to be open and transparent with our team to prepare them for what could happen. This way there wouldn't be any surprises. The worst-case scenario was that we couldn't give our people the bonuses they might have earned under normal circumstances, but because we set things up that way, it meant we wouldn't have to start cutting people if the situation became dire. That's a fair tradeoff for everyone. Our people are paid well, and bonuses are an extra reward for their hard work, but they aren't guaranteed. For them to make money, the business needs to make money, and when it does, everyone wins.

There is always a potential crisis looming on the horizon, and as we write this today, that potential crisis is inflation. We have no idea what will happen, but we will not panic. However, being in such a competitive marketplace, we must watch what's happening, especially on the service side. Not all of our cost is labor. We have the cost of the vehicles, fuel, insurance, and a slew of other expenses. We didn't raise our rates during COVID and always try to minimize rate increases or hold off as long as possible, but sometimes that isn't possible. After the pandemic, we needed to offset our costs and catch up on our service margins, so we increased our rate and added fees for certain work order tickets and job site visits. Nobody was happy with the situation, but everyone understood that was the cost of doing business in today's marketplace. Everyone wants to focus on rates, but we try not to get caught up in that and instead focus on the value we provide our customers.

We've worked through different economic down cycles, so we're confident we can do it again. We don't know what challenges we will face in the future but will continue to thrive by working together as a team to come out on top. Of course there is always a little bit of luck involved, but our preparation and philosophy are what have carried us through tough times. That gives us stability and allows us to be flexible and invest at times when our competitors can't. We're always looking for opportunities to grow; if there aren't any available, we'll create our own.

> *Our preparation and philosophy are what have carried us through tough times.*

Since we opened our doors twenty years ago, we've become a bigger organization responsible for ninety people and their families, and the best way to take care of those families is by continuing to grow. We look to do that in both good times and bad.

C H A P T E R 7
CONTINUED GROWTH

When we landed big projects with the University of Illinois in 2005, that job became bigger than what we could handle out of the Springfield office ninety minutes away. We didn't want our people traveling too far out of that ninety-minute radius because that made it difficult for them to provide the customer with the necessary support and resources. We opened an office in Champaign to support the university and that general area. It's since grown into a hub of sorts that has created other opportunities. Opening a new field office is an excellent way to grow our business, but the conditions need to be right for it to work.

> Opening a new field office is an excellent way to grow our business, but the conditions need to be right for it to work.

In 2018 we got a call from the regional director at Schneider Electric asking if we'd be interested in talking with an organization in Middleton, Wisconsin, whose owner had tragically passed away a year earlier. It was a family business, similar to ours, and after losing the founder, key employees stepped up to lead the business. Together with the remaining employees, they held it together for a few years, but the family wanted to sell.

We were actively looking to grow the business, and this would let us expand into Wisconsin. We didn't want to go too far outside of our general area, and what was great about this opportunity was that this company was located very close to Illinois. That put it within the same distance as our other offices. It also catered to the same type of customers we did—schools and healthcare facilities. There was a good synergy there, so we decided to pursue the opportunity.

We met with the family in June to begin negotiations and do our due diligence. Thanks to Frank's background, knowledge, and experience selling and acquiring branches back at Invensys, we could use the same process. We dusted off the asset purchase agreements we had used to establish the joint ventures and closed the deal to purchase the branch in Middleton, Wisconsin, in October.

The former owner told his employees they were selling the business on a Friday. We showed up at the farmhouse in Wisconsin where the business operated on Monday to meet the ten remaining employees and show them the presentation we had prepared. We didn't want to lose anybody, but there would be some changes. This company had done its own installations, and we would subcontract that work out, so we didn't need that side of the business. We didn't want to lose any customers either, so we immediately communicated the change to them as well.

The first step was to implement our systems and processes because they didn't have much of a system. The key people were used to doing everything themselves: going on service calls, putting in quotes, ordering and picking up materials, and keeping track of all the paperwork. We wanted them to run things independently but within the guidelines we provided. They needed to comply with us, not the other way around. That meant we had to train everyone on how we ran our projects and operated the service business. Everything changed, from accounting to how they reported their time and documented all their work. We even transitioned them over to start installing Schneider's new technology.

It was Zach's job to get those remaining employees integrated. He was responsible for implementing the acquisition plan and did a great job working with their people locally to get everyone on board. Old habits die hard, but we had been here before with our own team when we first took over the branches. We knew that some things would get worse before they got better, and we knew that was necessary if we really wanted to change the system and get them doing things our way. Some employees retired, including the owner's son and brother, who weren't looking to stay involved in the business. Marty and Justin were key local leaders with great customer relationships that we needed to continue with the business. Others weren't a good fit for our culture. We then added some new technicians, engineers, and service people. We also built up our Rockford-based engineering team with the idea they could be mentored by Phil back in Illinois to support the Wisconsin office. It was slowly coming together, but it didn't happen overnight.

It wasn't easy for those employees either. The transition required trust on their part, and we provided support virtually from our Rockford office while they assimilated. Once they realized they would be taken care of and saw that our systems and processes made things more efficient and easier for them to do their jobs, things went smoothly, and they were on board.

The employees were just one of the many moving pieces. We needed to establish relationships with local subcontractors in the area and modify our internal reporting to track our performance in

Wisconsin. The office was located in a different state, so we had to start paying Wisconsin taxes and set up payroll, withholding, and all that fun stuff. It took a little over a year to get everything rolling, but overall the process was pretty painless.

Today everything is integrated, up to date, and running smoothly, so the Wisconsin office follows the same execution model as all our other offices. We've even started training one of their guys to become a project team leader. None of this would have been possible if we hadn't gone through the growing pains years earlier when installing those systems and processes. Marty and Justin's local leadership and customer relationships combined with Alpha's operating and business systems were the glue that held everything together and allowed us to expand and grow.

Schneider has encouraged us to expand into Wisconsin, and we have a few customers in the Milwaukee area. We are about two or three years behind where we started when we set up in Champaign, so the circumstances aren't the same, and achieving that same level of success will be a new challenge for the Alpha team. We can do a lot of this work remotely, but to truly be effective, we need to have the core team to support and serve the customers on the ground.

That's what we're in the process of doing, and it starts with modernization. We're trying to move our current customers in Wisconsin over to the new EcoStruxure, which is Schneider's current offering, and we're getting good traction. We're working with a school district and landed our first energy-solutions project. The idea is for potential customers throughout the state to see the energy and utility savings they can earn with our latest technology because that makes our value proposition much more appealing. It takes time to plant those seeds, and it all goes back to having patience because we can't try to do too much too soon. Whether opening another field office, finalizing a new strategic acquisition, or achieving organic growth with our core businesses, we need to be strategic with how we invest our resources and money.

Growth is managed through the efforts of the team. Our team members in Springfield and Bloomington have earned new responsibilities and in turn have delivered quality growth. Through the local leadership of Jeff Miller, Jake Heigert, and Mitch Karr, we have improved the service and deliverables to our existing and new customers. Dan Reed was promoted to provide more local leadership and create more bandwidth for the Bloomington market.

ENCOURAGING THE NEXT GENERATION
By Zach Rotello: Chief Operating Officer (COO)

I've been with Alpha going on seventeen years now. I started right out of college as an entry-level field technician and had no real industry experience. I got to work on larger projects in the Rockford area, which gave me a crash course in how the business worked on the ground level. I got to see how the projects were put together and executed. It was an excellent foundation for me to learn how building automation worked and what it truly meant to provide value to the customer.

After eight years I transitioned into service management. While learning what it meant to provide value to the customers as a field technician, this new role allowed me to develop our processes and technologies to improve how we deliver those services to our customers. The inclusion of service software improved those processes, and going completely paperless made them more efficient. Leveraging technology to create lean processes and bringing in top-performing employees are what made all the difference. That is what's most responsible for our growth as a company. On the mechanical service side, we brought in some excellent refrigeration pipefitters with great experience who helped us expand our customer base and what we could offer those companies. We had two mechanics when I started in that role, and now we're up to sixteen. After five years in service management, I moved into overall operations and have become less focused on the service side of the business and more involved in the overall operations, so there are a lot of different projects under my wing.

I learned early on how getting the right people in the right roles increased our profit. That's why we rely on the Culture Index to determine if they will be good for the role and fit in naturally with what we're trying to do or if they will have to modify their behavior. We try to look for people with a strong work ethic and a desire to learn and who will put in the time to learn and ramp up quickly.

Bill Gantz, the field supervisor for central Illinois, is another example of a dedicated employee who came over to Alpha in 2003 with the purchase of the Springfield branch office. Bill was key to the growth and profitability in central Illinois by utilizing his expertise and industry knowledge supervising project installations. Bill reached out to me with plenty of notice that he was going to retire in a few years. You do not replace a veteran like Bill, so it was extremely important that we developed a succession plan to replace Bill. Working with Bill, we were able to identify individuals in Bloomington, Springfield, and Champaign who were hired, and, with Bill's assistance training the new team members, we were able to have a smooth transition and continue to support and serve the customers in central Illinois.

I really enjoy being able to develop some of the young people. Many are just like me and came in without industry experience. These are smart people who are good communicators. David Kleckler in our Springfield office came from the insurance industry, so he had some management experience. He knew nothing about building automation or HVAC but quickly ramped up, learned our industry in that control engineer role, and moved into a project management role. David is doing a great job, so I'm excited to see how he continues to grow.

Steve has been in a project management role in the Champaign-Bloomington area for many years, and we moved him into a senior role, so he could use his years of experience to help develop these younger guys. One way we do that is by creating a feeling of safety within the culture, so people aren't afraid to make mistakes. If you have to do one hundred things, I'd much rather you do ninety-five of them right and five wrong than do only five perfectly. That means our employees can work without fear of getting disciplined or yelled at. They know they will be supported. There's a difference between making the same mistake repeatedly and getting things wrong the first few times you do them. The latter is the only way to grow, which is why I'm a big proponent of autonomy that allows our employees to challenge themselves in a safe environment.

In the end I think that's what sets Alpha apart, and the proof is how so many of our current employees were referred to the company by family and friends who worked with us. We rarely have to rely on recruiters or pay referral fees to find quality people. The reason is that we've developed a reputation for treating our employees right by creating an atmosphere of collaboration and fairness. Fairness is one of the benchmarks that Frank and Brent constantly preach. Everyone treats each other and the customers the way they want to be treated. I've come to value that more and more the longer I stay with the company.

IS THERE SUCH A THING AS TOO MUCH GROWTH?

Our growth has been steady—16 percent in 2018 and a record 26.4 percent in 2019. In the last five years, we doubled the business and averaged 15.2 percent growth, which is on the high end of quality growth, which we consider 10 to 15 percent.

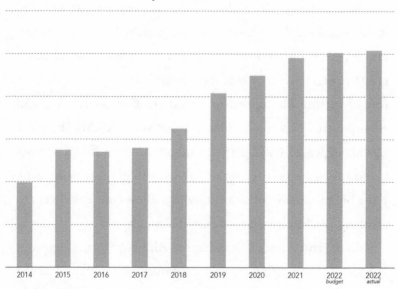

Alpha - Total Revenue

We've been able to achieve our growth the past two years while one of our largest customers had to hold back on new developments due to the impact of COVID-19. This customer pretty much shut down during COVID, so there will be a backlog of opportunities for us when it gets up and running again. However, during this same period, there has been a significant increase in negotiated, teamed-up, and customer-executed work on its campus.

We could not have predicted how much we have grown over the last couple of years. Then again, in the beginning we didn't think we could grow bigger than a low-end double-digit-million-dollar business. When we did that, the train just kept rolling, and we have now surpassed all those early expectations.

If we had to boil down how we did it to one word, it would be "impatience," specifically impatience with things that have always been done the same way. It may sound cliché, but we're constantly

> *If we had to boil down how we did it to one word, it would be "impatience."*

looking at every aspect of the business to see where we can become more efficient. None of this is pie-in-the-sky stuff. There is a formula. We must remain nimble and be willing to adapt to drive quality growth via continuous improvement that allows us to provide innovative solutions to our customers. That builds the trust required to maintain long-term relationships with them and also our vendors, subcontractors, and stakeholders. We like to say, if we have been doing something the same way for the past ten years, we need to change it because we are not leveraging technology and our team's new abilities to our greatest extent. That is "impatience"!

Our culture is about investment. We don't skimp in that area. It doesn't matter if it's a new technology, training, physical resources, or adding employees, if it can help improve our business, we will look to add it. We're never resting on our laurels or standing still. Not every change will work, and of those that do work, not all can be implemented overnight. At the corporate level, there was an expectation that significant change could be deployed in a month or a quarter, but the reality is that some changes take years to implement. That's why you must stay the course. With that attitude nothing is impossible. Instead of saying, "We can't get this done," we always find ourselves asking, "How can we get this done?" When you have the right people, the impossible suddenly seems possible. That attitude has gotten us far, but that doesn't mean we don't have a ceiling. We've frequently exceeded expectations because our team is phenomenal.

Looking back over how we accomplished more than we ever set out to achieve, it's easy for us to want to move faster than the organization allows us to move. It's a good problem to have, but it's still a problem, and we must ensure that we don't fall into the trap of getting too far out over our skis.

In the old days, we would probably have said that we'd be in dangerous territory if we were growing at 10 or 12 percent a year, but things have changed. Our business is very labor intensive, and we have quality systems and standards that allow us to grow well beyond that—even 20 percent during our best year. When there is momentum within the organization, our eyes can get bigger than our stomachs, but that's when we make sure to be the most patient with ourselves and our rate of change. That can be difficult when we're excited about something because we always want to see how far we can take it, but we must continue to be selective with the projects we pursue and focus on prequalifying our customers, so we can maintain those ideal profit margins. By investing and leveraging technology, quality growth is not a forecast or wish; it is a reality that will happen.

Quality growth requires being in control—in control of what we have in our backlog and what we're bringing in the door. It involves being able to execute with our current team and making sure we have the people in place to complete jobs on time and on budget as we continue to grow. The more we grow, the more difficult it becomes to bring in the people needed to match that growth because it requires us to be overstaffed. It takes a year to get a new employee up to speed and two to three years to get them working at total capacity, so they can take on their own projects, like our senior people. So if a new opportunity presents itself and we don't already have the people in place, it's too late. We must add new people before we need them in the field, or we won't be able to satisfy those customers. Our ability to do that has made our growth possible.

New employees are the lifeblood that helps us better serve the customer, so we're always on the hunt for quality people. We have contributed to scholarships for a program organized by Rock Valley College and Northern Illinois University to help students earn a four-year engineering degree for $40,000, which is unheard of. We need engineers, and we want to retain our local talent, so we gladly accept interns from this program. They learn about our systems, processes, and technology. It's an excellent way for us to develop talented people. After their stint with Alpha, some move on to bigger companies and pursue different opportunities, but we leave the door open if they ever wish to return.

In 2017 we had fifty-three employees, sixty-eight by the end of 2020, and ninety today, of which only five were with us the first day we opened our doors. We've even added software engineers as we continue to invest in analytics to help automate, streamline, and enhance what we're doing on the project and service sides of the business. It requires a lot of work by our internal team to bring those people up to speed in such a short period, but that's a testament to the processes and systems we have in place.

Our employees will always be our number-one asset, so we invest in their development. It's humbling to have so many people pick Alpha as the company where they want to begin and advance their careers. As we've grown and bolstered our customer-focused project teams, we've had to rearrange some of our key team leaders, and they continued to thrive in those new positions. We're so proud to watch these individuals move up in the company, and we want to provide career pathways for all our team members if they choose to pursue them.

A big part of our ongoing growth is taking the development of our people to the next level by getting a system in place and establishing different training tracks, depending on each employee's path. Whether they want to become a project manager or go into business development, we can provide the training to get where they want to go within the company. Just like we're transparent with our employees about the company's financial goals, we want to do the same with their career trajectory, so they know where we're going as a company and how they fit into that plan. During the pandemic we got away from our professional development reviews, but that's something we're looking to bring back. The chart below shows how quality growth is directly linked to our employees. We have been able to add team members to support business growth while increasing revenue and maintaining gross profit per employee.

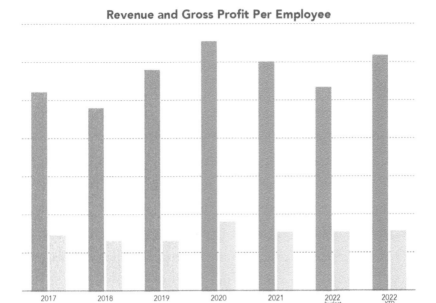

Revenue and Gross Profit Per Employee

THE FUTURE OF ALPHA CONTROLS & SERVICES

When we started, the goal was not to grow the business. We wanted to serve our customers, develop our people, and enhance our processes. Through doing that we couldn't help but grow the company. That growth is inextricably linked to how well we serve our customers, and those two things can't be separated. It's now in our DNA to grow, so we always have an eye toward the future, whether that's possible acquisitions, expanding into new markets, building out our leadership team, or restructuring the organization. We're at a place now where we can have those conversations, but they are no longer conversations only between the two of us. When we started we were a fraction of the size we are now, so the two of us could keep our fingers on everything, but that's no longer possible. That's why we share our strategic vision with our core team of experienced and capable leaders. It's why we've developed Zach, Phil, Andrew, Mike, Dan, and Jason. We've given them more responsibility, and they've all stepped up and worked together exceptionally well to take over running the day-to-day business.

One reason that's possible is because we partnered with a professional employer organization (PEO) to handle many of our accounting and administrative functions. As we've expanded the business into Wisconsin and some of our people have started working remotely in different states, things have gotten complicated on the administrative side, and the PEO helps ensure we remain in compliance. With the PEO's help, we can offer our employees more benefit packages and a series of choices more common in a larger organization. It also does payroll, processes the payroll taxes, and provides HR support. These were all things we used to do ourselves, but we didn't know what we didn't know, so we could have easily gotten ourselves into trouble.

With our new leadership team in place, the two of us can take a step back and provide support and coaching while ensuring our talent is being developed and our resources properly allocated. We keep tabs on the investments we've made to ensure we continue to reach that target of 10 percent growth each year. We meet with our directors monthly and work closely with our partners to maintain that productivity.

Alpha Analytics has become a significant part of our strategic vision for the future. The industry has been trying to get into analytics for a long time, but it's been a difficult sell. The technology doesn't always resonate with the customer, and some offerings are too sophisticated for our marketplace. Some universities have embraced analytics and incorporated these tools into how they manage their facilities, but they aren't always an integral part of the systems customers want.

However, with the cost of these software solutions going down, we can start incorporating more of this technology into our service offerings because it's such an efficient way for us to oversee and manage our customers' systems. If you have a school district with two dozen buildings, analytics is a great way to monitor the schedule of each building to cut down on energy costs. This is especially beneficial for the customers that are short-staffed and not replacing the employees who were the most familiar with these systems. It keeps us closer to the customer and allows us to provide better all-around service. Whenever we automate our processes, we don't have to apply our labor, so the customers get more value. Once they see how many man hours can be saved with analytics, they better understand the benefit of leveraging technology, and we can provide services they finally want to purchase.

With the cost of energy rising, our energy-solutions business is becoming an increasingly crucial component of what we do. Much like COVID shined a spotlight on proper building ventilation, high energy costs made customers want to make their buildings more energy efficient, so they could cut their utility costs. That involves curtailing usage during peak demand hours, so they aren't running their equipment at times when they could incur substantial price increases. Our systems can manage that output by limiting

> *Everything we do is in constant review.*

equipment usage and electrical load during those timeframes. That cuts costs and helps them earn utility rebates when possible.

We're always working with Schneider to learn how to do things differently and more efficiently, but we also have to follow the market and understand what our customers need to better help them understand the value of what we offer. That's the key to the engine that drives our growth. Meanwhile everything we do is in constant review.

We're always comparing where we are to where we were and tracking our progress with the rolling forecast to ensure we meet our growth targets, so we know where we can improve and ways to increase our profit. Ultimately if we don't have profit, we can't reinvest in the company and our people. That's the fun part, but it's also essential for our succession plan.

We want to build a multigenerational legacy business that remains true to our core values. We want the culture we created to live on and thrive. When Invensys was selling the branches twenty years ago, many of the people who bought them were looking to make money so they could retire. That's what many of our peers are doing now. The two of us never thought of it that way. We didn't want to retire early. We wanted to build something that could make a difference in the lives of people who work for us and have fun doing it, so this has been a dream for us. We dove headfirst into this endeavor and constantly talked about how to grow and protect the business but never once discussed what to do when this dream was over or how the company would survive if one of us ever wanted to retire.

In 2018 we finally had that conversation. That's when we drew up and set in motion a ten-year succession plan that involved Frank transitioning his 50 percent of the business to his son, Zach. It will still be a Bernardi and Rotello business, just with a different Rotello.

Under any other circumstances, this would be a recipe for disaster. There are reasons some companies have rules against nepotism, and those who do pass their business onto the next generation typically don't survive. A generational succession plan is not something we initially planned for or ever took lightly. It's a decision that evolved over time, and it's the best option for us.

Jason has been with us from the beginning and was instrumental in helping us grow the business and develop the Alpha team. We couldn't ask for a better cultural fit. He's intense, focused on the customers, highly motivated, and a great communicator, and he sets high expectations for our team. As the other directors have grown in their leadership positions, they also look at the business from a leader's perspective, which allows the entire team to focus on the Alpha mission statement and quality growth.

Zach is forty as of this writing and has been with the company for seventeen years. From the very beginning, he knew that he had to prove himself. That's why he never mentioned his last name when introducing himself to others when he started. Frank made it a point to treat him like any other team member and not be any harder or easier on him. And during his seventeen years with the company, he proved to be a good fit and quickly adapted to the culture. When he demonstrated his ability, he moved up and was given more responsibility. He stepped up and took much of what we did to the next level. He and Mike worked together to automate some of our systems and processes, so they could quickly ramp up new people to be more productive. That's been incredibly beneficial for that team and the company as a whole.

Bill Gates once said, "I choose a lazy person to do a hard job. Because a lazy person will find an easy way to do it." The real point of that quote is that Gates wants people who find a better way to do things because it saves time and makes everyone more productive. Zach is able to look at something and find a better, more efficient way to do it. He's always looking ahead to the future and is a lot like us in that regard. He doesn't want to be doing the same thing repeatedly if he doesn't have to. He wants to make the process as simple and lean as possible and watch it continue to evolve. And just like us he does not micromanage the team members. The employees respect what he does and follow his lead. He believes that getting the best out of people involves giving them the necessary support and then stepping back, getting out of the way, and letting them do their jobs. That's been our ticket to success, and he buys into that. He has good judgment and makes sound decisions that have proven his ability to lead.

None of the organizational changes we've made has occurred by accident. Our business has matured to where the excellent leadership team we've developed over the years can focus on the organic growth of the core business. They meet regularly, and the two of us sit in periodically on those meetings to ensure we're on target and moving the business forward according to the work plans. We give them all the rope in the world but still hold onto it lightly, so we can yank it if we need to. Now that he's strategically and slowly stepping back, Frank can focus on the bigger picture but has definitely found it hard to let go. Whenever he asks why he wasn't in the loop on something, we have to remind him that it was because it wasn't something strategic. He's no longer supposed to be looped in on everything, which takes some getting used to.

Brent is ten years younger than Frank but knows he will need to one day have that conversation about who he hands his half of the business to. The good news is that we have a plan and process laid out that can be implemented when the timing is right to transition Brent's ownership.

> We're at the point today where we don't want people coming to us with problems.

We're at the point today where we don't want people coming to us with problems. We want them to go to Zach, Andrew, Jason, Mike, Dan, and Phil because they are the next generation, but acclimating requires them to make mistakes. That's not only okay, but it's also important. You can't protect your kids from every bump and bruise because they'll never learn anything. They must fall off their bike if they're ever going to learn how to ride. We give our input and try to push them in the right direction, but sometimes not having things work out is the best way to learn. If they aren't about to make a catastrophic mistake, we let them go but make sure to pull them aside after the fact and show them why it's better to do things differently. It's the best way to learn, and what every one of those new leaders has in common is that they all want to learn. We're lucky that they have all embraced that role. It's so satisfying to sit back and watch this team follow our lead and pick up where we left off to take Alpha Controls & Services to the next level.

CONCLUSION

C ompanies talk a lot about culture, and you can say you have a culture, but it doesn't matter if you don't live that culture. Our employees have purpose and drive. They take pride in what they do, but, most importantly, they live our culture, which has made all the difference. We think that culture is not enough because it's everything!

Everything we do in our business and the success we achieve is a direct result of our culture. You can draw a straight line from everything we do to our core belief system. First we take care of our customers because without our customers we don't have a business. We must treat our customers fairly, and that means treating them the way we want to be treated. Think of how many problems in the world would go away if people treated others the way they wanted to be treated. For us that isn't hard because we've had great customers and built many lasting friendships with them over the years.

Second, we make sure to take care of our employees and treat them fairly because without our employees we wouldn't have a business either. Treating our employees fairly means providing them the career opportunities to grow, so they can take care of their families. The two of us benefited from growth opportunities at Barber-Colman, and that allowed us to do what we do today. We make sure we do the same thing with our employees.

This isn't new. We didn't make up what we do out of thin air. The two of us are doing things we learned throughout our careers from some brilliant, experienced people who told us what was important and what to watch for. We're all products of our environment, and the two of us are fortunate to have been in an environment with people who really cared about their business and making it successful. That's what we replicated, and we've loved being able to work with each other to bring this dream to fruition. It's been a blessing and an absolute blast. We're different people and often see things from a different perspective, but we complement each other and work together very well because we share the same vision and values. However, Alpha's success is not about Frank and Brent. It's about the whole team.

We're so excited by what we've been able to accomplish as a team over these past twenty years, and we're thankful for every single one of our team members (past and present) because they are the ones who have made this success possible through their commitment to the company and dedication to our customers. We've said it a thousand times, but our competitors can have the same processes and technology, but they won't be able to achieve the same results because they don't have our employees.

What we do is very simple. We make buildings comfortable, efficient, and secure. And we don't just mean access controls anymore; we're also talking about analytics, energy efficiency, and cybersecurity now. With Schneider Electric as our partner, Alpha is on the leading edge of providing cybersecurity technology and energy-efficient smart solutions for our customers. This is a huge deal in our customers' world, and we do this job well, and we do it responsibly. We also provide best-in-class service. That's the standard we set, and it means a service call isn't done until the paperwork is filed, the invoice is sent, and the money is in the bank. We've worked hard to fit all these gears together so the Alpha machine can run smoothly.

When we look back on all the jobs of the past five years, we performed better than we expected. We've consistently made a little bit more profit on projects because we have a system, efficient standards, and processes. That's precise, and it's a very important control mechanism within our business because it means that we know our cost structure and what it takes to complete a project. It means we can accurately measure the potential risk while adding new people and implementing new technology. In the beginning, we set out to be consistent, and these numbers prove that we're accomplishing that goal. Even Schneider is surprised that we can operate that consistently. And our numbers are getting better each year as we take on more work and complete it more efficiently! That allows us to grow and reinvest in the business. Our service business is growing, and the only reason it isn't becoming a more significant percentage of the overall business is that the revenue on our projects also continues to grow. They feed off each other and allow us to offer more solutions to our customers.

Neither of us can believe twenty years have passed since we had that conversation in the Seattle airport about buying the branches. We don't have a crystal ball. We can't see what challenges the future holds, so we can only focus on what we can control. That means continuing to work together as a team to provide best-in-class service. It means ensuring we have a substantial backlog and bring in the right type of projects. It means adhering to the values and the vision that have gotten us this far. It means treating our employees and customers fairly. If we do that, the sky is the limit. We can only go upward. It's exciting to think about where we can take the company. We doubled the size of Alpha in the last five years, and we want to challenge ourselves to do the same again.

ABOUT THE AUTHORS

FRANK ROTELLO

The chairman of Alpha Controls & Services, Frank is a forty-year veteran of the HVAC and controls industry. He earned his BS in accountancy from Northern Illinois in 1975 and his CPA certificate in 1978. Frank's twenty-four-year career at Barber-Colman Company/Invensys Building Systems consisted of various executive management and financial positions. He is a past president of InsideIQ (the International Alliance of Building Automation Contractors) and participates in local community nonprofit organizations while serving on various boards and committees. Since 2015 Frank has served on the board of The Workforce Connection (local workforce board for Winnebago, Boone, and Stephenson counties), including a four-year term as the board chair.

BRENT BERNARDI

The CEO of Alpha Controls & Services, Brent is a thirty-eight-year veteran of the HVAC and controls industry. He earned his associate of applied science from Rock Valley College in 1982 and his BS in electrical engineering technology, with a minor in business, from Bradley University in 1984. Brent's nineteen-year career at Barber-Colman Company/Invensys Building Systems consisted of various engineering, marketing, and branch management roles. He held several executive management positions, concluding as the VP/general manager of North American operations. He has served multiple times as president of InsideIQ. He is president of his church congregation, is treasurer of the local United Way board, serves on the executive committee on local park district and community college foundations, and participates on other local boards.

ACKNOWLEDGMENTS

We are thankful to our spouses, Susie Bernardi and Janet Rotello, for the love and support they have provided us over the years. We are grateful for their dedication, which has allowed us the time to focus on creating a great business, while trying to maintain a work-life balance so our families could grow and prosper. We are truly blessed to have such wonderful partners in our lives.

Alpha is not alone in its journey to create a strong employee- and customer-focused culture. There are many businesses we have encountered in our professional careers that have encouraged us on our path and influenced our actions. We want to acknowledge those many great small businesses that are focused every day on taking care of their customers and employees and giving back to their communities.

Thanks to the Advantage|Forbes Books team for their professionalism and hard work. Their guidance and expertise were instrumental in helping us tell the Alpha story.

GET IN TOUCH

Your building is our business. From energy management to building automation, boilers, chillers, airflow management, power monitoring, and building analytics, we keep it all running smoothly, making your facilities secure and efficient and you and occupants comfortable.

Website: www.alphaacs.com

Corporate office:
4104 Charles Street, Rockford, IL 61108
Phone: 815-227-4000
Fax: 815-227-4004
info@alphaacs.com

Find us on social media:
www.facebook.com/AlphaControls/
www.linkedin.com/company/alpha-controls-&-services/